FLIGHT FROM FEAR
A Rabbi's Holocaust Memoir

Rabbi Samuel Cywiak
With Jeff Swesky

2nd Edition

Flight From Fear: A Rabbi's Holocaust Memoir (2nd Edition)
Copyright © 2010 by Rabbi Samuel Cywiak, Jeff Swesky
Copy Editor Nancy Quatrano

Cywiak, Rabbi Samuel
Swesky, Jeff
    Flight From Fear: A Rabbi's Holocaust Memoir
    200p. 47ill. cm.
    ISBN 978-1-937100-00-1
    1. History – Holocaust – Non-Fiction – Memoir. I. Title.

Dreamer Publications, LLC.
www.DreamerPublications.com
(904) 207-8560
Printed in the United States of America

For my father, Baruch Cywiak, whose sacrifices made it possible for me to survive the Holocaust and have an extraordinary story to share with the world.

For Grandpa Cywiak and my mother, Rebecca Lasco-Cywiak. The love, faith, and wisdom they showed throughout my early years stayed with me, helping me to get by the dark days of the Holocaust.

For my late wife, Malka Cywiak.

For the six million Jews murdered during the Holocaust.

Acknowledgements

Rabbi Samuel Cywiak would like to thank:

My friends Dr. Roger J. Geronimo and Anne and John Byner for all they've done over the years and continue to do to help and support me.

The following doctors and physicians who have taken such wonderful care of me during my years in St. Augustine: Dr. Shriram S. Marathe, MD (Nephrology & Internal Medicine,) Dr. Edward H. Scarpitti, MD, (Urology,) Dr. Bruce R. Witten, MD, (General Practice Medicine, Ear Care, Neurology,) Dr. Stuart A. Soroka, MD, (Gastroenterology,) Dr. Howard Baker, MD, (Cardiovascular Disease & Internal Medicine,) Dr. Robert Gerson, (Optometry.) They are a big part of why I'm still here at the age of 90.

Author Jeff Swesky would like to thank:

Rabbi Cywiak for giving me the opportunity to ghostwrite his Holocaust memoir and trusting me with such an important and personal story.

Karen Harvey for announcing this opportunity and introducing me to Rabbi Cywiak in the first place.

My mother and father, Donna and Walter Swesky, for their undying love and support over the years, and for Mom's reviews of the early versions of this manuscript.

My sister, Tracie Arnold, and my cousin, Caroline Wiest, for being my biggest cheerleaders.

The Rogues Gallery Writers, Michael Ray King, Rebekah Hunter Scott, Bridget Callaghan, and Nancy Quatrano, for all the advice, insight, feedback, and laughter on this as well as other projects. Additional thanks to Nancy for an incredible final edit of this manuscript—your instincts were always spot-on. Also, additional thanks to Bridget for the amazing portrait she took of me, which now graces the back cover.

Both the FWA Ancient City Chapter and Ruby Tuesday Table 609 critique groups for their excellent critiques on various chapters, which were key in guiding me to properly write such a complex and dynamic story.

Additional thanks to:

Howard Orenstein (horenstein@mcdaniel.edu) for helping to obtain permissions for some of the Wyszków photos we wanted to include. Howard helps to maintain the website "Explore Your Jewish History in Wyszków, Poland":
http://www2.mcdaniel.edu/Psychology/HBO/JHWyszkow3.html

Lance Ackerfeld for his assistance in obtaining digital photos of Wyszków, Poland from the Hebrew book, *Sefer Wyszkow.* Information on Lance's organization, the Yizkor Book Project, can be found at: http://www.jewishgen.org/Yizkor/

To all the friends, family members, and fans who have loved and supported us over the years. Our apologies for not being able to mention you all by name.

Author's Note

Writing the name of "The Holy One" is not prohibited by Jewish law, but defacing or erasing it is.

To prevent the written Name from being defaced in any way, observant Jews will avoid writing it in any form, regardless of the written language. Instead of writing the Sacred Name, Orthodox Jews will replace letters or syllables with other characters. For example: "The L-rd is our G-d."

This practice will be honored within the text of this book.

G-d Bless.

Contents Page

Introduction

I survived the two worst human monsters in history: Adolf Hitler and Joseph Stalin. In 1939, they became allies and divided Poland between them. These two ruthless dictators had a lot in common. Hitler built a concentration camp in Auschwitz in 1940, and many more later. He is credited for murdering over twenty million people, including six million Jews. One and a half million of those were children.

Stalin's Auschwitz was Siberia, where people could not survive more than a few years in the frigid temperatures. Tens of millions of people died in Siberia, mostly Christians. Stalin did not discriminate based on religion. *Anyone*—including the refugees who escaped to Russia—who did not agree with Communism was sent to Siberia.

Since I was young, strong, and single, I found ways to survive grim situations and avoided falling prey to either Auschwitz or Siberia. Stalin was in power for several decades, so he had more time to kill millions more than Hitler. In a span of nearly thirty years, Stalin exterminated up to thirty million people. Considering the records kept by Soviets are incomplete and not completely reliable, some feel the figures could be much higher.

Just imagine if Hitler was in power for even one more decade, how many more innocent people would have died.

Flight From Fear

Part I

German-Occupied Poland
(August 1939 – December 1939)

1

One windy morning in the waning days of August 1939, I stood pensively on the train platform in Baranowicze, Poland, suitcase in hand, waiting for my train.

I was nineteen, and for many years had been studying abroad at different "yeshivas," rabbinical seminaries, preparing to become a rabbi like my father. I was to become a seventh generation rabbi, a very proud family tradition.

Surrounded by heavy pine forests, Baranowicze was a key railroad junction between many major cities. It was also the home of the Hasidic Slonimer Rabbinical Seminary, where I was officially enrolled. I studied at the local non-Hasidic yeshiva as well, to get a broad and complete rabbinical education.

Since the locale of my education was nearly two hundred fifty miles from my "shtetl," a small Jewish village, I could only afford to return home and see my family once a year. My shtetl was on the Bug River in Wyszków, Poland, approximately thirty-five miles northeast of Warsaw, our country's capital.

I returned around this time every year to prepare for, and participate in, Rosh Hashanah, the Jewish New Year, which concludes ten days later with our holiday, Yom Kippur. These are the most solemn and important days of the Jewish calendar.

But this year was different.

Pages of a newspaper blew across the platform. I watched them drift quietly away and knew they contained articles about Germany's continued efforts to cause terror throughout Europe. The Nazis had already overtaken Austria and Czechoslovakia, which were our neighboring countries, so an invasion of Poland seemed inevitable. We just didn't know when.

I must've become transfixed on those fleeing pages, because I jumped when I heard a girl shout my name.

"Shmuel, Shmuel!"

I turned to see a young, thin girl with dark brown hair run toward the platform. As she came closer, I recognized her pretty face.

"Rachel?"

She greeted me with a tight embrace.

"What are you doing here?" I asked though part of me was glad to see her again before I left.

"I don't want to see you go," she said, desperation in her warm, brown eyes.

"But I have to go. We talked about this."

"Why? You're heading right toward the Nazis! Warsaw will probably be one of the first places they'll target . . . and you'll be right there." She buried her face in my chest and began to cry.

"Listen—my family is back there," I said with a forced calm. "I have to go back to them and see if I can convince them to return with me."

"Can't you reconsider? And stay here with us instead?" I had celebrated the "Sabbath," the Jewish day of rest and worship, with her family, for years now. Her parents, whose house was right across from the yeshiva, treated me like a son of their own.

"No, I must return and see to my family's safety."

"But you could get killed."

"I promise to be careful, but I have to leave."

She looked at me with doubt. "Will I ever see you again?" she asked, tears streaming down her cheeks.

"I certainly hope so."

As the steam engine's whistle screeched its departure, I watched Rachel through the passenger car window. The train lurched forward and slowly chugged along the tracks. Rachel ran alongside, waving with a pained look on her face. I waved back and watched her shrink away and eventually disappear from my sight.

I felt a terrible emptiness.

We had grown close in recent years. She seemed to be falling in love with me and I was very fond of her as well.

Every Friday night in the great hall at my yeshiva was a segregated celebration, where the male students would sing and dance, while the girls would have to sit up in the balcony above and watch. Some nights, I would signal Rachel, and we would sneak from the synagogue and sit on a park bench or the front porch of my apartment and talk about our future together.

Now I didn't know if I'd ever see her again.

After I arrived in Wyszków, I walked through town toward home. An open market existed right off the streets not far from our apartment. There were many kiosks around and people filled the market, looking to make purchases.

Today, I found my mother, Rebecca Cywiak, at a booth. She made crafts to sell at the market during the day while the children were at school. This was necessary to help my father take care of our big family; I was one of seven children!

"Mama," I exclaimed and hurried over. We embraced.

"Oh Shmuel, I'm so happy to see you!"

"Me too, Mama, me too."

The market was beginning to shut down, so I helped my mother gather her things and walked her home. I lugged my suitcase and she carried a large basket containing various knickknacks.

"Is that basket heavy, Mama? Want me to take it?"

"No, son, I'm fine."

We returned to the U-shaped, two-story apartment building where my family lived. The heavy iron door, which was the only entrance into our complex, was wide open. At night, it would be shut and locked, because thieves were around, looking for things to steal. Thanks to the respect and admiration many had for my father and grandfather, we lived in one of the safest places in Wyszków.

During the day, the public could come and go as they pleased. The landlord, a wealthy Polish man who owned the entire complex, ran a long bar located to the side of the door and faced the street. He was in a good location for that. We were on Rynek Street, the central street in Wyszków, so many people would pass by and they could order a drink right there from the street. Behind the bar were tables and chairs and even pool tables, so customers could come inside and sit or play a game of billiards. The apartment overlooked a courtyard where the children living there often played.

We passed through the entrance, past the tavern and its patrons, and entered the hallway leading to the apartments.

"Here, Mama, you look tired. Let me take your basket."

"No, Shmuel, it's okay."

But her weary frame told me something different. "Mama, please. Let me help."

"You are such a good son—how can I say no?"

She handed over the basket and we took the staircase to the second floor where our small apartment was located. I could tell the worry of invasion was draining her.

My father, Baruch, returned from the Hebrew school, the "Talmud Torah," with my three youngest brothers, and they welcomed me home. I had already been living away from home at the yeshiva before my brothers were old enough to get to know me, before the youngest was even born. Sadly, I felt like a bit of a stranger to my own family. Since the age of nine, before I even reached Bar Mitzvah, I had been living away from home dedicating my life to G-d.

Later, I sat in the living room speaking with my father, while my mother was in the kitchen and my brothers played in the bedroom. My father was the principal of the Hebrew school and was in charge of 1,500 children. He also taught one class, but mainly handled the day-to-day operations of the school as well as hiring other teachers.

Not a tall man, my father was stocky with thick, strong arms. Honoring Orthodox traditions, he had grown sidelocks and wore a long robe. His red beard was long and full like an upside down evergreen tree. I was studying at both Orthodox and Modern Orthodox yeshivas, but I leaned toward the latter. I was clean-cut; no sidelocks, no beard, and I dressed conservatively.

I heard someone at the front door, and thought it may have been our water delivery; my mother was waiting for it so she could cook dinner. We had no running water in the apartment—common for small towns—but there was a public well in the middle of the street to use for drinking, cooking, and bathing. Boys from the shtetl brought pails of water to the house for a fee. They made a living this way.

With no running water, our toilets were big pits that were dug behind the apartment complex. Inside our complex, we had a room on the first floor with buckets inside. Every time we had to go to the bathroom, we went in one of these buckets, and then had to carry the bucket to the big public toilet and dump it in. Our room of buckets was better than going to the bathroom at the public toilet, because the smell was terrible and you had no privacy with apartments all around.

I started to get up, but the door opened. It was my sister, Nehama. She had just returned from the local Bais Yaakov, which is like a yeshiva for girls where they study the "Torah," the first five books of the Hebrew Scriptures. It's not so they can became a rabbi, but to learn to lead a religious life.

"Nehama—look at you!"

"Welcome home, brother!" We greeted each other with a hug.

"Still living at home? When are you going to get married?" I teased her.

"Is that why you came home, so you can give me a hard time too?"

"No," I laughed. "I'm only joking with you. I was just telling Papa how crammed it is here. I'm used to having my own bedroom at the yeshiva!"

I had a point—our home was a one room apartment for the seven of us, and it was even worse when my older brothers were still at home. My oldest brother, Label, had married and accepted a job in another city and lived in a different shtetl. My third oldest sibling, my brother Nahum, lived and worked in Warsaw. Nehama, the second oldest behind Label and eight years my senior, and my three younger brothers, were all still living at home. They had a lot of needs and were a big responsibility for my parents.

We were poor. A rabbi didn't get enough of a salary to take care of a big family. My parents slept in the two beds, and all the boys slept on the floor around the beds. My sister slept in the living room and had a curtain around her bed to provide some privacy.

This is why my brother, Nahum, was the only one in the family who was not very religious. He realized the life of a rabbi would be a poor one and he couldn't take it. Instead of studying the Torah and working to become a rabbi, he moved to Warsaw, the capital of Poland, and started doing anything he could to make a living, and survived very well. He was also a football player in Warsaw, where all the best players from Poland could be found. He was not like us, but he did what made him happy.

Nehama flashed me a grin letting me know she understood.

"See, Papa, she understands. Nehama has no privacy here."

"Son, I have a story to tell you." My father smiled. "There was a widow, who lived in a small one bedroom house with her six children and their family dog. How could she live like this? It was terrible, right? She didn't even have a husband to help out anymore.

"So—one day, she visited the rabbi. She said, 'Rabbi, I don't know what I'm going to do! I have six children and a dog and only one bedroom. How can I survive like this?'

"The rabbi asked, 'What about animals, do you have any animals outside?'

"'Why yes, Rabbi, I have a bunch of goats, so that we can have milk and make cheese. But they're not my problem!'

"He said, 'Look here. You'll have to listen to me, okay? You came to me because you think I can help you. No matter if you understand or not, I'll tell you what to do. But just listen and *do* what I say.'

"'Okay, Rabbi, that's why I came to see you. I need your help!'

"'All right. I want you to take all the animals *inside* the house, one by one, take them all in. Understand?'

"'Okay, Rabbi, I'll do as you say.'

"She took in all the animals, and a month later she went back to the rabbi and said, 'Rabbi—it's terrible! I don't know how I can survive one more day like this!'

"He said, 'All right, all right. I know, I know it's terrible. Don't worry about it. Take the animals back out.'

"She takes the animals out and AHHHHH, she sighs of relief. Very good! Life again! Things were back to how they were *before* she visited the rabbi, but this was after she experienced something even *worse*. Suddenly, living with six children was not such a bad thing after all. You see? The lesson is—things can always be worse."

"Hah!" I laughed. "That is a good lesson, Papa. I'll be quiet now and enjoy what we do have, okay? You don't need to bring any goats up here—I've learned!"

"Are you sure? I could probably go find some!"

"No, no—not necessary." My smile faded as a more serious topic came mind. "Papa," I said. "Why do we have to wait here? Why don't we flee like Jabotinsky told us to do?"

Ze'ev Jabotinsky was a right-wing Revisionist Zionist leader and founder of Irgun, an underground militant Zionist organization. Jabotinsky urged all Polish Jews to evacuate Poland for Palestine as soon as possible. He had studied Hitler and read *Mein Kampf*, so he knew what we'd be facing. During a speech in 1938, Jabotinsky said we "were living on the edge of the volcano."

"Where do we go, son? To America? America is not a land for religious Jewish people."

"How about Palestine?" I asked. "We can be Jews, religious Jews, in Palestine."

"No, you do not understand. We must stay here and wait for Messiah. He will come soon, we don't know when, but it could be any day. So we are obligated to stay here and wait."

"But if we are going to wait for Messiah, why don't we wait in Palestine? Why do we have to wait here?"

Sometimes I asked my father questions he didn't care for, because maybe it seemed I had less faith in G-d than he did, or more to the point, less faith in his "rebbe," a Hasidic leader. But he did not correct me. He let me ask these questions. He was careful with me, because I was so sharp.

My older brother who became a rabbi was Hasidic, like my father, but I was different. I was a "misnaged," *opposed* to the Hasidic beliefs, because my main yeshiva was that way.

"Only Messiah can lead us to Palestine, son. And only then can we start building a state of Israel. We cannot believe that Hitler is going to do what he said he's going to do. G-d is not going to let him do it."

I knew this was a common belief among extreme Orthodox rabbis. My father was an Orthodox rabbi and was following the advice of his Hasidic rebbe, the Gerer Rebbe. The Hasidic rebbes were believed to have a "Spiritual Vision" from G-d. This vision was that we would be protected from Hitler by G-d. Jabotinsky, although he was Jewish, was not considered to be religious, so the

Hasidic rebbes would not listen to him. But I was young and inquisitive, and Jabotinsky's warnings made more sense to me.

I noticed my mother at the edge of the kitchen area, listening to our conversation. No longer occupied with dinner preparations, she wrung a kitchen towel with her clenched fists.

"Mama, tell him we don't have to stay," I said.

She met my gaze, but quickly lowered her head.

"We have no choice, son, but to stay," my father answered for her. Her shoulders slumped as she turned away. But not before she dabbed her eyes with the towel.

2

The next day, September 1st, 1939, we received news that Germany invaded our country; it was declared the start of World War II. Warsaw, our neighbor and the capital of Poland, had already been targeted by German bombing raids. We could hear the distant rumblings of war.

Several days later, on September 5th, I sat by the window overlooking the courtyard and studied the "Talmud," the collection of ancient rabbinic writings consisting of the Mishnah and the Gemara that constitute the basis of religious authority in Judaism. I began singing the words like a song. And a realization hit me.

My grandfather, who had lived in the apartment next to us before passing away several years earlier, used to do the same exact thing. He would get up very early in the morning, when everyone was still asleep, and study the Talmud. Every morning for hours.

As a "cantor," a Jewish official who leads the musical portion of a service, he had a beautiful singing voice and used to sing the words of the Talmud aloud to remember them, to let them soak into his soul.

"This should be the right way to study the Talmud," he once told me.

The owner of the apartment complex, who was a Pole, had two sons. The youngest son, named Tajick, used to ride his bicycle around the courtyard every morning. Even by that time, my grandfather was still singing the Talmud. Tajick rode in circles around the courtyard and could hear my grandfather sing. He tried to imitate my grandfather, but did so in a cruel, mocking way. Making fun of him. Maybe he was influenced by some of the anti-Semitism around the neighborhood. The Jews and Poles were living together in Wyszków, after all. Or, maybe he was just being a bad boy; he was only thirteen years old.

One day, when he was riding around yelling aloud, mocking my grandfather, he rode out of the complex still poking fun. He biked down the street towards a big bridge that crossed over the Bug River. When he got to the bridge, he had an accident. Fell over and into the water, and got hurt. He almost drowned!

People need to be very careful about how they speak of others. Once an insult leaves your mouth, it cannot be taken back. You cannot fix it. It's already done the harm. One of the lessons my grandfather would chant was from the scholar Abiya. Essentially it had to do with speaking ill about other people.

Abiya said, "It's similar to eggs. When you buy a carton of eggs, you're very careful. Because if you drop the carton, the eggs could break! If an egg breaks, you cannot fix it. Same thing with your words. Be very careful with what you are saying."

My grandfather was well respected. He was considered to be a sage and a very holy man. A lot of the local Jews, who knew what was going on, said that G-d had punished Tajick for making fun of such a great rabbi.

I was lost in the memories of my grandfather when I felt the first vibrations. It didn't even dawn on me what they could be. They became stronger until, it seemed, the entire apartment building was shaking.

I jumped to my feet sending the chair crashing to the floor. Nehama dropped the book she was reading and stared at me. My mother approached us with her mouth agape.

"It's starting," she said.

At that point, distant explosions sounded and I could hear the buzz of planes approaching. My father and my three young brothers were at the Hebrew school.

We left the apartment and hurried to the street. Panicked people screamed and ran in every direction. The three of us headed for the trenches. People of our community had dug the trenches for protection against the predicted German bombing runs. I jumped into the deep trench, in order to catch my mother and sister to keep them from falling. We joined many others and we all huddled together in the cold, muddy earth.

I had seen small planes before, but nothing like these large, powerful German bombers. Dozens of planes filled the sky like bats bursting from a cave. They roared overhead, swooped down low, fired rounds, dropped bombs on houses, anything to scare and intimidate us. And they did. Many of us were gasping and crying out. We held each other close, and I felt my mother and Nehama shuddering against me.

Explosions started to sound off all around us. Homes and businesses smoked and burned from the incendiary bombs dropped by the German planes. At one point, I stood up enough to look around. I was worried about the rest of my family. I saw a woman, heading for the trenches, mowed down by a machine gun burst from a plane. She dropped to the ground with a lifeless thud. Others were shot as well. A man ran from a burning building, his clothing ablaze. These scenes filled my vision, one after another.

Now that the bombing had started, more people ran for the woods than the trenches. My heart feared that a bomb could find its way into the trenches, but we were still safer than the risk of being blown up or burnt in our homes or on the streets. And the woods did not offer much more protection.

All I could do was pray to G-d for His protection.

Hours later, when the last explosion had long passed and the drone of aircraft faded away, we realized the first attack had ended. One by one we got up and climbed from the trenches. I helped my dear mother and sister from the trench. My ears throbbed and rang from hours of constant detonations. People's voices, their shouts and screams, were muffled.

But it was over . . . for now.

Those remaining headed for their homes. Some who had fled for the woods returned, but the majority did not come back. It seemed they decided to leave for good; abandoning their homes and family to flee to another city. But where would they go? Would they be any safer?

As we walked, people coughed and choked while moving through walls of black smoke. Some stood around sobbing and mourned the lives of unlucky loved ones. Others stared in disbelief at the charred remains of where they once lived. I surveyed the area to find that many homes and businesses had already been destroyed.

We returned to our apartment to find that our building had been spared. Structures were burning all around us, but we were lucky.

Shortly after, Papa came in with my brothers. All of us exchanged hugs and well wishes. I gave my father a big embrace and hugged all of my brothers.

We knew that our lives would never be the same again.

3

For a couple of days the remaining members of our community headed for the trenches when the sounds and warnings of approaching bombers began. Each time we lay side-by-side with family, friends, neighbors, and strangers curled into balls, our hearts pounding, waiting out another attack. And attack they did, a few times a day they came and unleashed their bombs one after the next, sometimes, for hours.

On September 9th, I kept waiting for the planes to return and resume their bombing raids. As the day passed on, it became clear they were not returning. We knew it could not be over, so we waited with fear in our hearts, praying to G-d for His mercy.

Later in the day, I heard loud rumblings and the ground vibrated beneath my feet. I ran outside and saw powerful tanks and armored vehicles made of black steel barreling towards us. As the vehicles arrived, the German infantry wearing pale gray uniforms, spilled into our city. I kept my distance, but watched with great anxiety. Many ran in fear to hide.

Entering our city in a formation behind the German soldiers was the dreaded SS unit distinguished from the German infantry by their black uniforms and swastika armbands. The Nazis! Once a city or territory was taken over, the German army stormed off to the face the next battle, while the SS took over the local occupation.

The German army's goal may have been to win the war, but the SS—as we would soon learn—was more concerned with the eradication of the Jewish people. They were committed to wiping out any, what they considered, "inferior" people or races, such as minorities, gypsies, and homosexuals. Even the Polish population would eventually become a big target for these executions.

The SS soldiers grabbed our townspeople, pushed them, and knocked them to the ground. They shouted out the question, "Jude? Jude?" The German word for Jew. Those who nodded their heads or responded "Yes" were immediately beaten or shot. The shock of these acts penetrated my soul, my eyes burned. I was helpless to do anything to help.

I turned and ran home.

That night, there was a loud pounding at our door. My mother ushered Nehama into the bedroom to be with my brothers. Once they were out of sight, my father opened the front door. A Nazi lieutenant and a squad of his SS soldiers appeared on the other side. Donned in their menacing black uniforms, the lieutenant entered our house followed by two soldiers, their high black boots smacked against our wood floors. The lieutenant wore a German Luger holstered to his belt and the helmeted soldiers carried rifles.

"Cywiak," hollered the lieutenant. "Baruch and Shmuel Cywiak!"

He had asked for my father and me. We knew that some of the anti-Semitic Poles, as well as some local Germans, were working with the German army to inform them about the Jewish leaders in our community. Anyone the Germans might perceive as a threat. So, it was only a matter of time before they came to look for my father, a well-respected rabbi and a teacher at the Hebrew school.

My father stepped forward first, and I, with some hesitation, followed him.

"What do you want from us?" I asked.

My father told me to keep quiet.

"Where are you taking us?" I demanded.

The only answer I received was the crack of a rifle over my head by one of the soldiers. I collapsed to the floor. Pain shot through my head, my eyes watered. My father helped me to my feet.

"We are taking you on a work detail." The lieutenant looked to my mother and then me. "There is no need to resist. If you do, you'll only make it worse. Come quietly and there won't be a problem."

The soldiers grabbed and shoved us out the door. They jabbed us in the backs with their rifles as they marched us into the streets. My heart raced. Just what were they planning to do?

Outside, our community's rabbis, teachers, and leaders stood in a big group with worry evident in their eyes. Maybe more than sixty men in all were standing in the street surrounded by groups of soldiers and officers. I was the youngest by far. All the rest were our town's elders.

We were about to die. I felt it in my gut.

They marched us through the town, across the long bridge over the Bug River, and out into a field towards the woods on the other side of the river. A couple Kuebelwagens, similar to the American Jeeps, drove beside us for the officers. Along with the headlights, a few soldiers carried lanterns to light the way. The whole time my mind was occupied with trying to find a way to survive. There was no help, nowhere to hide.

My father took my hand and held it tightly. We walked side-by-side, shoulder-to-shoulder. Thank G-d my grandfather, Papa's father, had passed away several years earlier, or he would have been on this fatal march alongside us.

My father leaned close and whispered, "Son, do anything necessary to survive. You may be the only one of us to live. Don't go back to the house. Run, run as far away as possible. Try to get to Russia if you can. Promise me you won't give up."

"Okay, Papa."

But what could I do? If I tried to run, they would gun me down, kill me right then and there. My mind raced as I tried to think of something, anything, which would get me out of this nightmare. To save myself.

But while my mind raced, I continued moving along with the rest of the group towards certain doom. At the edge of the woods, the soldiers stopped us in front of a long, shallow pit, which they, or a group of Poles, must've dug out a short time earlier. The lieutenant shouted in German as the soldiers shoved us around until we formed one long straight line facing the pit. Our backs were to the soldiers with the toes of our feet close to the edge of the pit.

I peeked back and saw the soldiers lining up behind us readying their machineguns. This was it. I faced forward and prayed. The clicks of their rifles cocking echoed through the night. My father pulled me close to him. Everything was happening too fast—what could I possibly do to get out of this? I looked to G-d, knowing that He would ultimately take care of all of us.

The lieutenant barked out an order and I heard the soldiers raising their weapons. My father squeezed me against his chest. Another order and the cracks of the machineguns began to sound off. *Rat-tat-tat-tat-tat.* My father shoved me into the pit and I crashed against the cold dirt. I looked up to see others dropping lifelessly into the pit. They had us facing the pit, so we would easily fall into it once we were shot. Or perhaps they didn't want to see us and have our faces, the faces of the dead, come back to haunt them in their sleep, their nightmares.

Moments later, my father landed beside me. I dared not speak to him. In the faint light, I could tell that my father was dead. A splotch of blood appeared just below his shoulder.

Then I realized that had been his plan all along. One to save my life. I closed my eyes and played dead as bodies continued to fall and fill up the pit.

After some time the shots lessoned in frequency, until they stopped altogether. The lieutenant, in a less intimidating voice, gave a command and I heard their boots stomp off through the grass taking with them the dim light from the lanterns.

As quietly as possible, I rolled my father on his back to find a large exit wound in the middle of his chest pouring blood. He must've been shot straight through the heart.

The engines of the Kuebelwagens started up and they drove away. And then, all was still and eerily quiet.

As I lay in that death pit, I cried for my father and for all the people who were just senselessly murdered. I prayed and prayed to G-d to have mercy on their souls, to welcome them into heaven.

When I knew the Germans were long gone, nearly an hour later, I sat up and looked around. The night was upon us and it was too dark to see any movement.

"Can anyone hear me?" I asked aloud. I waited for responses, but none came. "If you're alive make a sound and I'll come help you—." Still nothing. "Anyone? Anyone at all?"

Out of sixty or so Jews, all elders except for me, marched into the woods by the Germans, I was the only survivor. I was surrounded by death; the senseless murdering of Jews. This would be their final resting place, their grave. What kind of evil does these things? Such inexplicable hatred towards another culture.

"Oh, dear G-d, why is this happening to us?" I cried out to the silent night.

4

I laid there in that mass grave and wept. I wept for my father, for the other Jews who were murdered along with him, for a sacred tradition that would be no more—my time away from the yeshiva to observe the holidays with my father. As my heart broke and my mind struggled to cope with all the senseless death in that pit with me, I drifted back in time with precious memories of happier times.

In previous years, when I came home for Rosh Hashanah and Yom Kippur, I didn't stay with my family. My father and I would go to see our great Rebbe in a small town near Warsaw called Gera. We didn't even know his name. People used to call him the Gerer Rebbe.

There were a lot of Hasidic Rabbis in Europe, but our Rebbe was special. He had thousands and thousands of followers all over the world, who believed in him, who believed he was the greatest. That he was a prophet, a holy man.

It was expensive to go see the Gerer Rebbe. Only those who could really afford it went. My father would save all year just to go—he didn't have much of a salary from the community. My father was a rabbi, but not the rebbe of the people. There were over ten thousand Jews in the area, and in those days, there was only *one* rebbe, for the whole city. There were many rabbis with the education and titles to do the job, but only one could be the head rebbe. So what did they do? These rabbis went out and got other religious jobs.

My father got a job in Warsaw. He was one of the three people who founded Agudas Yisroyel. It was a big organization for real Orthodox rabbis and still exists today. They have branches in America and all over the world now. My father was one of three men who ran and managed that organization. He had an office in

Warsaw together with Isak Meyer Levine, the son-in-law of the Gerer Rebbe, and R. Benjamen Minz. Isak Meyer was the biggest speaker in the organization. It was exciting to hear him speak.

They were so powerful and strong in the capital that they had their own daily paper for all of Poland. Isak Meyer wrote for it occasionally, my father wrote every Friday, but Benjamen was the main writer for the newspaper.

In his later years, my father couldn't go into the capital to tend to this job. He had to be home to help my siblings and me, because my mom couldn't do it by herself anymore; there were too many children to care for by herself. So he got a job as the principal of the local Hebrew school.

To be a principal of a Hebrew school of 1,500-2,000 children, you had to be a rabbi, had to be a learned man. My father was also on the board of directors for a Jewish bank that gave loans without interest. But these jobs did not pay well—it was difficult for him to raise a family of seven children on those salaries.

My father believed in the Gerer Rebbe very much—as did my grandfather. Thousands of people came to be with the Rebbe for the ten days of the holidays . . . from Rosh Hashanah to Yom Kippur. The tenth day from the first of the Jewish New Year is Yom Kippur, Day of Atonement. We had to stay the full ten days, pray with the Gerer Rebbe three times a day, and after the tenth day, we went home. This was our annual tradition.

The first thing we were supposed to do on the day we arrived was to get in a line to see the Gerer Rebbe, and say, "Shalom," our traditional expression of greeting or farewell.

My father told me once, "You better be good, because he can read your mind."

My father and grandfather truly believed the Gerer Rebbe was such a powerful prophet that he could read your thoughts.

There was a big synagogue hall where the services used to be. Five thousand or more followers would show up to see the Rebbe, but the synagogue hall couldn't hold all those people. There was a big field outside, but that was full too! At night, the followers stayed in various hotels, anywhere they could find room.

The big event during the entire ten days was the "Third Meal" on Saturday. The Gerer Rebbe would make an important sermon about the Portion of the Week, the reading from the Torah. There was also a big meal for everybody who could get inside.

In my early years when going to that event, I used to get a place before the third meal started. Hours before, I would get under the table and lay on the floor next to where the Gerer Rebbe sat. I'd end up being right underneath his legs. That way I could hear every word he said—I was learning something. He must've always sensed me down there, because he used to throw down food, like fruits and vegetables, figuring I was hungry. Not only did I hear his sermon, but I also got something to eat!

There were times, when I couldn't get under the table, so I would climb a pillar. To be able to stay up there and be comfortable, I would tie a rope around the pillar, put my legs through, and hang suspended there. I tried everything just to hear him. If you were very near, you could listen to the sermon. But if you were far away, even inside the hall, you couldn't hear, because he was a very old man, and he spoke softly.

There was a big long table, and the only people who had the honor to sit at it were important rabbis. My grandfather was one of them. When my grandfather got old and couldn't go any longer, my father took his place at the table and sat very close to the Rebbe.

There eventually came a time when my father could not stay inside, because of his asthma. He couldn't breathe very well inside that crammed hall, so he had to stay outside. By then, I was getting too big to lie under the table, so I stayed outside with him. I didn't want him to be alone.

He would stand near the windows, straining to hear the Rebbe, but he couldn't; it was impossible. Everybody knew it was impossible. The windows were very high, and when it was cold outside, the windows wouldn't even be open. But everybody stood there looking intently at the windows anyway, even though they couldn't hear.

So I asked my father, "Why do you try to hear, when you know it's impossible?"

He said, "Well, you don't know that. Maybe I don't hear with my ears, but my soul has a capacity to hear, so my soul is listening."

I couldn't say anything to argue with that reasoning.

Each major city had a chief rebbe. And they would be named after the town that they presided over. Our Rebbe lived in Gera, so he was known as the Gerer Rebbe.

In their system, they didn't have elections. But in a way, they were selected. Take a small shtetl where the Jewish people were poor, not learned or educated. They didn't have factories or big businesses in these shtetls; just small shops and the open markets.

If there was one intelligent, learned man amongst these Jews, he would act like a rabbi and would become famous, and these poor, uneducated people would begin to believe in him. He would become their G-d, in a way. The rebbe of the town. And once he was in, he was in for good. And would pass on the status of rebbe to his sons, like a monarchy.

The rebbes were not like our ancestors who had their education through "semichas," rabbinical ordinations, from yeshivas. No. They didn't even have seminaries—they studied by themselves. Before the war, some seminaries were developed, but even those were created and run by the rebbes; the ones *without* an ordination, without an election. Just because they were the smartest and wisest. And there were dozens of these types of rebbes. Even the Gerer Rebbe received his title this way.

There was a lot of controversy about whose rebbe was the best. People would be very emotional about their rebbe.

"Why does this rebbe claim that he's better than ours?"

"Why does he claim he's more important than all the other rebbes?"

The truth is no rebbe would claim such a thing. They were all much too humble. The "Hasidim," the followers of these rebbes, made these claims; they started this hatred between each other. Hasidim of one rebbe would hate the Hasidim of another.

There was another city nearby called Alexander, so they had the Alexander Rebbe. His followers were called the Alexander Hasidim. I was a Gera Hasid. And there was a hatred between the Alexander Hasidim and the Gera Hasidim. But this hatred was started by a handful of troublemakers, who spread rumors, and it soon became truth. These people felt offended by anyone who didn't believe in and follow their rebbe. They even made up Yiddish songs about how great their rebbe was over the others.

One I still remember. "Ours is the best—the rest are stupid."

I heard a rustling above the trench. I held my breath, blocked the memories. When the sound did not repeat, I let out my breath. Hatred was not limited to the Germans . . .

These rivalries are similar to European football. The football fans have their fight songs and get into rumbles with fans of opposing football teams. But this is not some sport; this is our religion!

The Hasidim feuds exist way back in our history. Because of hatred within our own religion the Second Temple was destroyed by the Romans. Our sages tell of a story where Emperor Nero became convinced that the Jews were rebelling against Rome.

A wealthy Jew was to host a party for his son who was getting married. The high priests of the temple and all the important people of the community were to be in attendance. The host of this party had a good friend by the name of Kamtza and an enemy named Bar Kamtza. Instead of the good friend, the host's servant invited Bar Kamtza by mistake.

Bar Kamtza took this as an act to make amends, so he dressed in his finest clothing and attended the party. When the host saw Bar Kamtza, he said, "Who invited Bar Kamtza; he's my enemy!" He told Bar Kamtza that he hadn't been invited and demanded that he leave immediately.

Bar Kamtza showed his invitation.

The host said, "It's a mistake, you're not invited! I don't want you here—get out!"

Bar Kamtza said, "Wait, I will pay for whatever I eat and drink."

This request was refused.

"Then allow me to pay half of the cost for this feast."

"No!"

"Then I'll pay for the whole party—whatever it cost—I'll pay. Please don't embarrass me in front of all these people."

The host did not accept and had him thrown him out into the streets. Angry and embarrassed, Bar Kamtza said, "Since the rabbis were present at the feast and did not stop him, this shows they agreed with him. I'll slander them to the Emperor!"

He went to Emperor Nero and told him that the Jews were making fun of the Emperor and were planning to rebel against the Roman kingdom.

The Emperor wanted proof.

Bar Kamtza said, "Send an offering to the Temple and see if it will be accepted."

A choice calf was given to Bar Kamtza to take to the Temple, but along the journey Bar Kamtza intentionally blemished the calf. He did this because he knew it would not be accepted in the state it was in.

Word got back to Emperor Nero about the refusal of his offering. He became enraged and ordered the destruction of the Second Temple of the Jews.

All this happened out of hate. Nobody said a word or did anything at the party to stop this hatred. Not the high priests, rabbis, or leaders of the Jewish community. So G-d said, "You have no leaders—you haven't learned a thing. You do not deserve to have a temple."

In the pit, beside my father's corpse, I remembered these things.

5

Hours after the shootings, when I knew it was safe, I said a final farewell to my father, and climbed from the pit. Against my father's warnings, I stayed in the shadows of night and crept across the bridge. I had to go back for my family, even if it was a major risk to do so. Across the horizon I saw Jewish homes in flames, the Nazis were destroying them all.

On the other side of the Bug River, I snuck back to our apartment building, taking precautions not to be seen. Since a Pole owned the apartment complex, it had been spared.

I crept back inside our apartment to find it empty. My mother wasn't there, neither were any of my siblings. There were no signs, no traces of them—they were gone.

I left our apartment the same way I entered, as if my life depended on my silence. I visited some of our Polish neighbors and lightly tapped on their door.

"Did you see my mother? My family?"

"Yes, they went to Białystok."

"Białystok?"

"Yes, the Germans have allowed Jewish women and children to leave town. Many have headed to Białystok to reunite with their families."

"Thank you. I need to go and find them." Białystok was a big Polish city approximately eighty-five miles northeast of us. It would be hard to locate them, if they were there, but I had to try.

"Good luck. May G-d be with you," my neighbors whispered.

I would later learn that the horrors for the people in Wyszków had only just begun. Sometime after my departure, the Nazis marched over five hundred Jews into the big Wyszków synagogue, locked them inside, and set it on fire.

After September 13th, Wyszków no longer had a Jewish population. We were all gone by one means or another.

⫟ ⫟ ⫟

As I headed off on foot towards Białystok, I wondered what my mother thought had happened to me. Was she told that we were all murdered out in the woods? If so, she had no idea that I had survived and was looking for her. If she believed that both my father and I were dead, how would she manage to keep it together while looking after my little brothers? I imagined my sister being strong for her, taking on much of the burden.

While traveling, I was so afraid of being found by the Germans, that I did most of my walking in the woods. I traveled near the edge of the woods so that I could see and follow the major roads to know where I was going. But aside from roads, there was nothing *but* woods; on both sides of the street and as far as the eye could see.

At night I slept in the trees. It was so awkward and uncomfortable up there, not to mention the danger of falling down while sleeping, that I never rested properly.

After days of walking, I was so tired and hungry that I went up to a house and knocked on the front door. They didn't have telephones in most homes, so I wasn't worried that they would call someone on me. There was not much chance of a German soldier being there. Germans wouldn't be caught out in the woods or at farms, because of the partisans. If they'd be caught alone without other soldiers, they'd be killed. The Germans stayed in the cities where they had homes and offices.

A Polish woman answered the door.

"Please, ma'am, please help me. I'm tired, and I haven't eaten in days."

"Oh, I'm so sorry. But I can't help you. I have a family. You understand? I can't risk getting caught helping you." She looked over her shoulder. "Well . . . wait here." She disappeared inside the house and returned a few moments later with a sack. She handed it to me. Inside were vegetables, fruit, and a piece of bread.

"I wish I could do more to help." Her eyes filled with tears, her chin quivered. "Now I must ask you to go away. Please, go away."

"Thank you for the food. G-d bless you."

A couple of days later, I came across a farm. It was a large piece of property with a house toward the roadside and a huge barn that sat much further back. It was night time, so I snuck into the barn. It was filled with farm equipment, stacks of hay, and many animals; mainly cows and horses. I curled up on a stack of hay and fell asleep.

The next morning, when the owners opened up the barn to begin their day's work, I hid toward the back. It was big enough for me to do so. I stayed in the barn a few days, sleeping on the hay at night, even sleeping some during the day, and sneaking out into the fields to retrieve fruit and vegetables from their crops and trees. I even ate raw potatoes. They were hard on the stomach, but I had to do whatever was necessary to satisfy my hunger. Plus I had to regain my strength, so that I could continue my journey to Białystok.

One morning, I was not quick enough when the barn doors opened; I must've still been asleep. Suddenly I heard a woman.

"Oh, no, you're going to get me killed! They'll think I was hiding you!" The color left her face—she was very afraid of the possibility of being caught by the Nazis for harboring a Jew.

"I'm sorry, ma'am. I don't mean any trouble. I just needed to get some sleep."

"You have to leave—do you want me to be killed? My husband, my children—they'll kill us all. Please leave, and don't come back."

I apologized again and left.

There were many times during my travels when I would have to go up to a house to beg for a piece of food or sleep in a barn or sneak food from the fields. It became my way of life, of survival.

Sometimes after getting a sack of food from a farmer's wife, I'd go around to the stables with the animals, eat it all up, and then lay down to sleep. In the morning, I'd knock again, especially if I knew she was a good woman and kind.

I'd say, "I ate everything up! Could you spare some more?"

It wasn't only me doing this; there were hundreds of thousands of Jewish people running from the Nazis. We all had to do what we could to survive.

There were plenty of good Polish people along my travels, who wanted to help, who truly felt bad for what was happening to the Jews. They felt sorry, even cried at times. Some went out of their way to help. They had good hearts.

Sometimes I felt sorry for them! They were so openly broken up, especially the women; they showed their emotions. The men were a little colder; too worried about their families.

Israel recognizes those non-Jewish people who tried to help Jewish people and children during the Holocaust. They give them the same honorary title of "Tzadikim," righteous ones, which is also used for great Jewish spiritual leaders and rebbes. These non-Jews were people with a heart, who put their lives on the line to help Jewish people. If caught, they could have been killed just as easily as if they went against the Nazis . . . and often times they were.

Usually I stayed away from the cities and remained in the woods, even if I was hungry, because there was too much of a risk of getting caught by the Nazis in the cities.

But if I couldn't find ways to eat in the woods, then my choices became clear. I would either die of starvation or have to take the chance of being caught to find food in the city.

6

After a couple weeks of travel and days without seeing German soldiers, I left the security of the woods when I came to a small town. I still had hopes of finding my family.

I thought I was near Białystok, but I didn't know for sure. It may have been Ostrów, which was still a ways from Białystok. Cautiously I walked through the town, just wanting to get past it and back into the security of the woods.

A kind Polish man approached me with a sack over his shoulder. "What are you doing walking in the open like this?"

"What do you mean?"

"You are Jewish, no?"

"I am."

"You're not from around here?"

"No, I'm from Wyszków. I'm looking for my family; the Cywiaks. Do you know the name?"

"I'm afraid I don't. You need to be careful, the SS are everywhere. They're putting all the Jews into the ghetto."

"I'm trying to get to Białystok."

"Good luck and stay out of sight." He reached inside his sack and retrieved a piece of bread. "Here—I'm sure you're hungry. I must go now. Be safe."

"Thank you, sir. G-d bless you."

I was tired and weak from travel, and too many sleepless nights. But the hunger seemed to overpower all else. I found a secluded spot in an alley and practically inhaled the bread. That little bit of food in my belly would go a long way to give me energy.

Intending to leave the town as fast as possible, I turned towards the main street only to find myself facing two SS guards pointing rifles at me.

"What are you doing out here, Jude?" asked one of the guards. I didn't have a beard or look like a typical rabbi, but they certainly recognized that I was Jewish.

"I was just leaving."

"Leaving? Leaving for where?" the other one laughed.

"You're not from around here, are you?"

"No."

"I saw you eating. Where did you get the food?"

"I had it with me," I said.

"So you're hungry, huh? Come here." I walked towards them and one officer slammed the butt end of his rifle into my stomach and I fell to my knees trying to catch my breath. "Are you hungry now?" They both laughed.

They drug me through the town towards the impoverished area, probably the former living area of the poor Polish population, a ghetto. There was a makeshift wooden gate with the sign "Juden," which is German for Jews, posted to it. Another SS guard opened the gate so they could bring me in. Just inside, one of them pinned a yellow Star of David on my chest. The word Jude was written at its center.

"You are not to remove this when in public under any circumstances. Understand? It's very important that you remember that."

I knew that if they spotted any of us walking around without their star, they would kill us on site.

"Go on now. Get out of my face, Jude."

Cautiously, I moved away from them. There were thousands and thousands of Jews walking or standing around crammed into this ghetto. We were confined to the area of the ghetto by barbed wire. Coils and coils of barbed wire lined every exit, every possible avenue for escape. There was no safe way to get out.

After several days had passed, I understood that the ghetto was only a temporary environment; they had something worse in store for us. Why did they keep us separate? Were they going to feed us? No, of course not. They had sent us to the worst part of town and took away our homes, our possessions, everything. They took our valuables. They did all this and sent us to the ghetto to die.

The ghetto was to keep the local Jews together—separate from the Poles and others—to make division and get us ready to ship to the death camps. The SS would oversee this operation; it was their job. Ghettos were a holding place. They were established while the camps were being built.

Aushwitz was the first death camp to be created. They didn't have enough camps or space in the camps, so they kept the Jews in the ghettos until the concentration camps were ready for them. And as soon as they were ready for them, they had the Jews shipped to the camps, to their deaths.

The German army used a lot of Jewish people for work; those who passed the first "selection." If they came across some of the stronger Jewish men and women, they would force them to work for the Germans to help with their war effort. The Germans could do anything they wanted. They were in control.

But in the ghettos, people were dying from hunger. They crammed us all in there, but didn't give us any food. The Jewish people baked in the ghetto; they had some flour and made bread. But they had very little; supplies were limited. They had a system to get a ration of bread.

The Jewish Committee tried to help keep us fed and hydrated, but it was not easy to get food and water. They had trouble getting supplies from the Nazis, and when they did, there wasn't much to go around. We had to wait in long lines for food. Everything was rationed out; only enough to keep you alive. And even that was not a certainty.

When hunger wasn't the problem, violence was. The SS would knock us over the head for nothing. For them to hit or shoot us was a part of their job.

In most ghettos, there was not much resistance. There were no arms to fight back with. There were a couple of exceptions in the larger cities. The most well known is the Warsaw Ghetto Uprising.

Many years later, I learned that the leader of that uprising, Mordechaj Anielewicz, the partisan and well known commander of the "Żydowska Organizacja Bojowa," Jewish Fighting Organization, was born in my hometown of Wyszków in the year 1919. His parents moved to Wyszków after World War I. During the summer of 1942, he began establishing an armed organization. It is believed that he spent much of that time in the woods of Wyszków building this resistance in preparation for the Warsaw Ghetto Uprising.

One day in the ghetto, I saw a young woman across the street holding a baby boy. The baby was crying and crying, and she could not get him to stop.

An SS guard approached her. "I'm sick of hearing this Jew baby screaming. Make it stop."

"I'm trying, I'm trying," she said with a look of worry on her face. "He's just hungry."

"Hungry? That's not my problem. Make him stop or I will."

"Hush, hush," she told her son, but the baby only cried louder.

"Here, let me take a look," he said and slung his rifle over his shoulder. He took the baby boy from the mother and held him up. And then he did something that will haunt me forever. He grabbed the baby by his feet and swung him against the wall of a building, the precious little head striking against the hard brick surface. The baby made no more sounds and was dropped to the ground.

"There," the Nazi said. "Problem solved!"

The mother knelt, rushing to the aid of her baby boy. My mouth hung open. Despite all the horror I'd already seen with my own eyes, I couldn't grasp that any human being was capable of this evil. With rage in my heart, I wanted him to pay for what he did.

Other Jews looked on with horror was well, but the fear that hung over the ghetto was paralyzing. The Nazis were so intimidating, so cruel, you had to mind your business or you could be the next to die.

Before I could even think of what I could do, the SS guard retrieved the rifle from his shoulder and shot the woman through the back of the head.

He began to look around, looking for an excuse to have another target to shoot at. People hurried away, not wanting to be the next one killed.

—✳— —✳— —✳—

I prayed and prayed for that baby and his mother. I prayed for all of us, that this barbaric treatment would end, but I didn't believe it would be over anytime soon.

The death of that baby, and the deaths of the 1.5 million Jewish children during the Holocaust, is a hard truth to swallow.

How could G-d allow such an atrocity? How could any of the Holocaust be fair? This question haunted me for many years. In time, through study and prayer and spiritual development, I have found some peace to that question. During the course of my service to St. Augustine, Florida, I wrote an article that I offered to the community to provide comfort for the hard things that happen in our lives. The atrocities are man's doing. But no suffering goes unnoticed by G-d.

"And they saw the G-d of Yisrael; and under his feet there was a form of a sapphire brick, like the very heaven for clearness," Exodus 24:10.

This sentence is complex. Undoubtedly, the unimaginable notion of "seeing" G-d refers to some aspect of divine glory, as the commentaries have already expressed. The allusion to the "Brick of Sapphire" begs for explanation. Why does the Torah mention this?

The Targum Yonason cites a "Midrash," in-depth commentaries and interpretations on the Hebrew Scriptures, which sheds light on this enigma. This brick is a reminder of the wretched slavery to which Beni Yisrael were subjected. The Jewish men and women worked side by side, tramping and treading the mortar.

One delicate young woman in the advanced stage of pregnancy miscarried as she was treading upon the mortar. The stillborn child became mixed into the brick mold. The terrible wailing of the mother ascended to the heavenly throne, whereupon the Angel Gabriel was dispatched to retrieve this "brick" and bring it up to heaven. It was placed next to G-d's throne as a memorial.

A profound lesson can be derived from this story. No incident is relegated to oblivion. G-d records every horror, regardless of who is affected. No tragedy suffered by his children is considered insignificant. Amid all of the tension and shouting, one young woman pathetically cried out. The angel made a brick from the unborn child, and G-d had it placed near his seat. Indeed, as the Midrash continues, that very night G-d smote all of Egypt's firstborn and the people were released from slavery. The Sapphire Memorial was the most fitting tribute to this young "Neshamah," Hebrew for soul, and, perhaps a consolation for the mother.

With this concept in mind, we may begin to confront some of the horrifying tragedies, we have experienced, both as individuals and as members of Am Yisrael.

And amazingly our sages express a similar idea. The Talmud in Avodah Zarah 3B, questions, what does G-d do in the fourth part of the day? The response is: G-d studies Torah with little children! Rashi, a French sage and genius, who is most famous interpreter of the Talmud, explains that this refers to children, who had died when they were yet young!

Horav S. Schwab, Z.L., applies this to our sages in a most poignant way. Imagine for one horrifying moment, the one and one half million Jewish children whose lives were so brutally snuffed out during the Holocaust. They were tragically sacrificed just as they were at the threshold of life. They are presently studying Torah with G-d, himself. They have a personal "Chavrusa," study-partner, with the Almighty! This is perhaps the meaning of the "Sapphire Memorial." G-d perennially remembers those who have experienced more than their share of anguish in life.

(The preceding italicized section, an article written by
Rabbi Cywiak, is printed through the courtesy of
The St. Augustine Record.)

7

I stayed in the ghetto nearly two months, but knew if I remained much longer, I could die. I began to develop a plan for escape. There was a Jewish man, who was able to get certain things. I saved up bread from a couple meals and gave it to him in exchange for a pair of wire cutters.

I waited until late one night when the weather was terrible. The skies were pounding rain upon the ghetto. I snuck through the ghetto and found a somewhat secluded place; no guards, no lights. I escaped by cutting through the barbed wire fence with the cutters and went back to hiding in the woods.

Once I got my bearings and direction calculated, I continued my journey to Białystok. I took off my yellow star and slipped it into a pocket. In the ghetto, I'd have been shot for not wearing it. Outside the ghetto, I'd be shot if I *was* wearing it.

After arriving at Białystok, I asked around for my family. I was told that a lot of people were leaving word for their family members. There was a big wall in the center of the city where people nailed up notes and letters hoping their loved ones would come to that location searching for them. I looked through all the letters, but nothing was posted from my mother.

I wandered around asking Jews if anyone was from Wyszków or knew the Cywiaks. Eventually I happened upon a family who knew my mother. They told me my family had passed through Białystok, but they were no longer here. I had just missed them. And these people did not know where my family had gone.

I figured they must have traveled to Łomża, Poland, which is where my mother's parents lived. I had spent a lot of time in

Łomża as a child, because I attended my first higher rabbinical seminary there. The yeshiva was grand and prestigious. I stayed with my grandparents when not at school.

Immediately I left Białystok and headed for Łomża to visit my grandparents and hopefully find my mother and siblings as well. It was another long, exhausting journey filled with more physical and emotional pain.

Nearly halfway into my trek, I came across a small city near Tykocin. On the outskirts of the city in a field, I found three large pits. Two of them were filled in with dirt. The third pit was left uncovered. Hundreds and hundreds of dead, decaying Jewish bodies filled the pit. Scavenger birds preyed on their corpses. The smell was unbearable and similar to rotting waste or the foulest of gases.

I don't know how long I stood teary-eyed looking at the pit, reminded of my father's death, and my near-death, but the horror of it tore me to pieces. Only people of pure hatred could do such things.

"They didn't stand a chance," a voice sounded from behind.

I spun around with my hands raised, my heart thumping.

"I'm sorry—didn't mean to frighten you," said a Polish man.

I nodded at him and lowered my arms. "What happened here?" I asked.

"The Germans came in on foot—just stormed in and starting killing Jews. They didn't even bother bombing first." He shook his head. "The ones they didn't march out here were either killed in their homes or at the synagogue."

"The synagogue?"

He simply pointed towards the town. "No Jew survived. Not one," he said before turning and walking away.

Further into the city I found the burned remains of the synagogue. Inside the charred, destroyed building were hundreds and hundreds of burnt bodies, skeletons. It was easy to figure out what happened here. The Nazis, to get rid of many Jews in one shot, packed them into the synagogue, barricaded them inside, and set fire to the building eventually burning all the inhabitants alive. The few who found a way out were shot just outside of the synagogue.

These would be scenes I would witness again and again passing through cities in Poland.

The rest of the city seemed abandoned. I said "Kaddish," prayers for the dead, and continued on my journey to Łomża.

The stench of the murdered stayed with me.

8

That night an unbearable hunger came over me and I realized I hadn't eaten in days. I was in the middle of the woods, no city in sight, no farms in sight. There were times when I was able to catch an animal and make a fire to cook it. On occasion, I came across wild blueberries; any little bit of food helped to keep me alive. But this time I was having no luck, and it seemed I needed food to even *continue* my journey. My energy was sapped.

If I were to fall to malnourishment now, all would be lost. I would more than likely be caught or die in the woods.

It began to rain, so I sat down on a toppled tree trunk under a thick tree, and rested. I looked around for berries, anything to eat, but found nothing.

A squirrel scurried up to me and stopped. I looked at it for a few seconds before my survival instincts took over and I lashed out with my leg and kicked it in the head. The squirrel flew through the air and landed with a thud. I hurried over and picked it up. It was stunned, but not dead, so I quickly broke its neck.

Everything was wet, so I couldn't even try to start a fire by using matches, if I had any. With fires, I had to be careful, because it would give away my position if I was within the range of German soldiers.

Regardless, I had no way to cook the squirrel, and had no idea how soon I would be able to. Typically, with Jewish law, it is not kosher to eat raw meat or meat that is not properly prepared according to the stipulations of our law. There is an exception, though. It is permitted to bypass the kosher customs if a Jew's life depends on it.

I sat back on the log and stared at the animal. My stomach screamed for nourishment. I found some thick tree branches and used them as crude knives to peel back the fur and skin.

And then I did the only thing I could—the only option left—I began to eat the raw and bloody squirrel meat.

There is a story to explain this exception to the kosher customs.

There was a widow who was poor and didn't even have a place to live. She had a son, who became very sick. She took him to the doctor, who said that he has to eat chicken soup to get better. She saved up what she could and bought a chicken to cook for her son. The chicken had to be kosher; had to have a liver and a gallbladder. It had to be a healthy animal. If the animal could die in the next day or two, because it was sick, then that animal was not kosher to eat.

When the widow was preparing the chicken to be cooked, she couldn't find the gallbladder. A chicken could not maintain proper health and live without one, so she feared it was not kosher. She went to the rabbi and asked if she could use it. The rabbi looked and saw that she was right, there was no gallbladder. If it never had a gallbladder, it was not kosher and she could not use it.

The rabbi listened to the woman's story and became very compassionate. What else could she do for her sick child? She finally saved up enough money to buy a chicken for him, only to find it's not kosher. The rabbi didn't know what to do. How could he tell her it's not kosher?

The rabbi licked the innards with his tongue and couldn't even taste any bitterness, which means there never was a gallbladder. He said, "You know what, take a lick and see, maybe you'll find some bitterness. I couldn't find anything."

The woman took a lick and couldn't find any either.

She said, "Oy—it's bitter!" It was a common saying at the time. She meant her situation was bitter, in crisis. You can have a sweet life or you can have a bitter life.

The rabbi took advantage of her response. He said, "Oh, it's bitter? Then it's kosher!"

He felt so bad for the woman that he used a trick to make it kosher. There's such humanity when rabbi's make decisions like this.

The law does say that if it's for a person's health, they can eat anything. Kosher or not. The Bible says you have to guard your health very closely.

If her son had to eat chicken and she couldn't afford to go buy another one that's kosher, what was she going to do? The law says give it to him. But she was so faithful, that she would have listened to the rabbi regardless. She didn't know the exception to the law.

A couple of days after eating the raw squirrel, I continued my journey through the woods towards Łomża. With the rustle of leaves, a man appeared from the brush.

I jumped back with my arms up, hands balled into fists.

"Shalom," he said. "It's okay. You're Jewish, right?"

"Yes, I am."

"So am I. My name is Raziel. I'm with others too. Why don't you come meet them?"

I calmed down and realized he was telling the truth, so we gave each other a proper introduction.

"I'm sorry. You startled me—I thought you were the Nazis!"

"Are you hungry? What kind of question is that—of *course* you're hungry. Come on, I'll get you something to eat."

I followed him deeper into the woods until we came across a campsite, where several other men sat around a fire cooking food. They were older than I was, but not by much. He introduced me to the others and invited me to sit down.

"We are organizing," another man spoke up, "as part of the partisan movement."

Raziel handed me a cooked rabbit leg, which I devoured after thanking him.

"How many men do you have?" I asked.

"Not many yet, only twenty or so, but we're growing stronger every day. We have some arms too." He held up a rifle to show me. "With weapons we can get anything else we need. If we go to a farm, they give us food . . . or we *take* it. We have the power to survive, the power to fight back!"

"We have to fight—it's our only option," said another partisan.

"No, that's not the *only* option," I said.

"Dying is not an option for me."

"I don't mean dying. I mean running. That's what I'm doing. It's what my father—may G-d rest his soul—wanted me to do."

That awful day flashed back into my mind. I thought we should've run before the Germans arrived; we made a mistake. Jabotinski was right; the rebbes were wrong! My father and the other Hasidim thought that the rebbes were prophets, so holy that they knew and saw the future. That they could read your mind. They believed the words spoken by the rebbes were the Words of G-d.

This was not true! They were just rebbes, that's all. Human like everybody else. I think my father probably realized this too and changed his mind while we were on the way to the pit. He could see that they were all wrong; how could he not?

A question jarred me back to the campfire conversation.

"You're a young, strong man. Why don't you take up arms with us and fight?" a partisan asked me.

I had never picked up arms. I was afraid to use them, didn't even know how. "No, I can't. I've dedicated my life to serving G-d. Killing for me is just the opposite. Besides, I'm looking for my family, and once I find them, I'm getting us as far away from this as possible."

"I understand. Well, you're welcome to stay with us as long as you'd like. Eat and rest up for your journey."

While sitting in front of the fire, eating the first decent warm meal in months, I reminisced about our tradition of Shabbat also called the Sabbath, which is the weekly day of rest in Judaism. While on the run, I could not observe most Jewish laws like the Sabbath. I couldn't keep track of days—everything was mixed up. I couldn't do anything other than what I had to do to survive each and every day. All the rest was secondary.

Before the war, we had always honored the Sabbath. Shabbat began on Friday at sundown and was observed until Saturday when the first three stars appeared in the sky.

Friday night we used to eat fish and chicken soup. Chicken soup was very popular. But that meal was only for Shabbat; we couldn't afford to eat like that through the week, because it was too expensive.

Saturday we didn't cook—it was against the law. And we didn't have the technology to keep the food warm. We used to make a "cholent," a dish, like a stew, with a lot of potatoes, vegetables, meats, and "kapusta," which was a Polish soup with either cabbage or sauerkraut. This was our special meal for Shabbat. You ate it at lunchtime next day.

Friday before sundown, you sent the pot full of cholent down to the baker. They put it in the bread oven and it stayed there the whole night. The next day at lunch, they'd bring it back from the baker when it was still hot. Every Jew cooked cholent for Saturday's lunch.

When I was a small boy, I had to take the pot to the baker's before sundown. I carried it by hand—a big pot for the whole family! The bakery was across the street from our apartment. It was a very wide, wide street. One time, I fell on the street and the whole pot of cholent poured out.

After that, Mother always used to tell me, "Be careful—don't fall. If you know you're going to fall, first put the pot on the ground so it doesn't spill out. *Then* fall! But don't mess up the food or we'll lose it and have nothing to eat."

Hah! How do you know that you're going to trip and fall? If you did, how would you have time to put the pot down first?

You couldn't, of course. This was a running joke she started, all because of that one time I lost the cholent on the street.

9

I stayed the night with the partisans and got some badly needed sleep. In the morning, they showed me how to make fire by rubbing sticks together, so I wouldn't need to depend on matches. I had breakfast with the men, said my farewells, and continued out on my own.

The night of food and rest with the partisans gave me the strength to get to Łomża. In the city, I found the same destruction that my hometown had suffered. Buildings burnt or destroyed from incendiary bombs, toppled trees and scattered debris, people weary and suffering.

Three quarters of the city was in ruin. I reached my grandparents home, which had been spared, and knocked on the door. This was a home where I had spent a few years of my youth while I attended the yeshiva in Łomża, which was only a short walk from their home. So many memories were behind that front door.

Only, instead of my grandmother, a Polish woman opened the door. Before I asked the question, I knew what her answer would be; my grandparents no longer lived here. And that's exactly what she told me. She had no idea where they went or if my mother had passed through.

I wondered what had happened to them all. Did my mother find her parents, and they all left together? Were they all captured? Killed?

My mother's father made a living by selling food and wine. He owned a grocery store with a wine cellar, but was not the only grocery store in the city. There were lots of them. He'd stay open until he had enough money for them to live off of, and then he'd close up the store. He didn't want to be competition for the other store owners.

He was an example of humble Jewish life, generosity that existed everywhere within the Jewish community a few hundred years ago.

Many years later, I would find out that my kind and humble grandparents were murdered by the Nazis.

I did not stay in Łomża long; a few days, maybe. I wanted to get back to my current yeshiva in Baranovicze. A long ways off—on the other side of Poland near the Russian border—but it was the only place I knew to go. Since my family knew I had studied there, I had hoped that they may have traveled there trying to find me.

By sneaking into an open compartment when nobody was looking, I hopped on different trains until I eventually got aboard one headed to Baranovicze. For the first time since leaving home, I would not have to walk to get to my destination. I was hopeful during my journey that I would be out of the hands of the murderous Nazis, once there.

I had spent my last seven years at the yeshivas in Baranovicze listening to lectures at least ten hours a day, six days a week. The rest of the time was spent studying the Talmud. Sometimes we'd have to stay overnight at the yeshiva because we had so much material to cover.

The Talmud was written in Aramaic; a very difficult language to understand. There were sixty-three books of the Talmud and we had to study them profoundly. In addition to the Talmud itself, we had to study all of the Talmud interpretations from the great scholars, like Rashi and the Tulcifers.

Rashi was a French sage and genius of the Talmud. His teachings from the Talmud and the Bible could be found everywhere—he was quite famous for it. He was able to make the most cryptic and puzzling passages understandable and clear.

The Tulcifers were grandchildren of Rashi, and their interpretations did not always agree with that of their grandfather, but they would always explain why their translations were different.

There were other great interpreters as well. Each generation would have its brilliant scholars, who offered their translations; and these were made into books. We had to study and learn all these different perspectives as part of our education to become a rabbi. I've remembered the lessons all of my life; they've been stenciled into my brain.

⊀⎯⤙⎯⊁

We had plenty of lecture on morality and ethics; how to be a good person and leader in the Jewish community. Every day for at least an hour, we had to study books on these topics. The base of all our studies was morality and ethics.

Arrogance was the worse trait you could possess in those days. Back then, people wanted to learn humility and they wanted their children to be humble. There were special books on the topic.

Our prophets and scholars taught that G-d hates arrogant people. Since we don't want to be hated by G-d, we want to work at being as humble as we can be.

Some of the rebbes were actually *too* humble. There is a story about two rebbes, who were on the same level, but one was much too humble. Too much or too little of anything is no good.

The humble rebbe visited the other to pay his respects. He said, "I am not like you. I feel like I'm just like my followers, a Hasid. Ordinary, not special. Not a man deserving the title of rebbe."

The other said, "Why do you say that?"

"I am a Hasid, I'm not a rebbe like you, so I have to tell the truth. I am nothing. I am really nothing."

"If you are nothing, why don't you tell them that?"

He left the rebbe and did what he said. Told his people he was nothing. And the more he insisted that, the more followers he would get.

He went back to the rebbe, and said, "I told them the truth. Now I'm more popular than ever before, because they really think I'm truly humble. How can I convince them I'm not so great?"

The rebbe said, "Wait a minute, don't overdo it--they may start to believe you!"

⊀⎯⤙⎯⊁

There was a Jewish movement in Poland called Mussar. The goal was to become humble; not arrogant. To be nice to people, and criticize yourself, not others.

Their rabbi used to give a sermon once a week. One time he told them, "I have something for you to do as soon as possible. Go to the pharmacy and tell them you want to buy some nails."

They did as the rabbi requested. The pharmacist said, "You want nails? In a pharmacy? Are you crazy? You can't buy nails in a pharmacy!" The pharmacist and other customers laughed at the students.

This was a lesson in humility. The idea was to *make* them feel ridiculous. If we went to a pharmacy, which was only for medicine in those days, and asked for nails, what would we look like? The people there are going to make fun of us.

That's exactly what their rabbi wanted. He wanted them to experience how bad it felt to be teased and laughed at. This is how they would learn *not* to do it to someone else, because they'd already experienced the embarrassment and ridicule.

That was the Mussar movement. They did a lot of work like this to make themselves look ridiculous, so they could appreciate humility.

10

When I got to Baranovicze, I went to see Rachel and her family, but their house was empty. It was apparent that they had taken what was important to them and left town. As I feared, Rachel, who had become such an important part of my life, was gone.

I visited each of my yeshivas, only to find them empty. My student friends weren't at the apartments and rooms they were renting.

Everyone was gone.

Not only that, the Russians now occupied the city. They had signed the Molotov–Ribbentrop Pact with Germany just before the start of World War II.

This was a non-aggression pact between the two powerful nations, which also partitioned Poland between them. The west portion went to Germany and the east to Russia. A mere sixteen days after Germany's invasion of Poland from the west, north, and south, Russia invaded Poland from the east on September 17th, 1939.

The Red Army attacked fast and defeated the Polish resistance quickly. Hundreds of thousands of Polish soldiers were taken as prisoners of war. And the 13.5 million Polish citizens of that region were declared by the Russian government to be Soviet citizens.

I stood outside my main yeshiva, a place I had worked very hard at in recent years. I spent so much time inside that it had become a special, intimate environment to me. It was my home. This great yeshiva I'd become so attached to over the years was now a ghost town.

I began asking around to find out what happened. I came across an elderly Jewish man who filled me in on the Russian invasion.

"They don't want any resistance," he said. "They're not like the Nazis—they don't care if you're Jewish or not, as long as you abide by their laws. You are a Russian citizen now, and if you make problems you could be executed. Thousands and thousands have already been deported to Siberia and other parts of Russia to do slave labor. Where are you coming from?"

I told him about my experiences to this point and he shared his sympathy with me.

"This here was my yeshiva. Do you know where they went?" I asked.

"Ah, yes! They moved your yeshiva to Lithuania. Vilnius."

Vilnius, the former capital of Lithuania, was located near their border. After a history of turmoil, where the ownership of the city changed hands frequently following World War I, Vilnius and its surrounding area was finally annexed by Poland on February 20th, 1922.

I would learn later that the head of our yeshiva found out that the Balkan countries, Lithuania, Latvia, and Estonia, would remain neutral throughout the war based on the pact between Russia and Germany.

Poland decided to give Vilnius back to Lithuania to be on friendly terms, and that would keep Vilnius neutral as well. That's exactly what we needed!

The Jewish United Appeal, a United States organization that supported Jews abroad, helped organize the move of many yeshivas from war zones to Vilnius. Our yeshiva and many others needed a place like this; how else could we get away from the war and still study to become rabbis?

Immediately, I knew I wanted to be with them, so that I could be in a neutral place with my school, and be protected.

Before working on a plan to get to Vilnius, I walked around looking at the yeshivas, synagogues, and other spots that I had frequented in my days in Baranovicze.

There were two rabbinical seminaries in Baranovicze, one was Hasidic and the other non-Hasidic. I had studied at both.

The non-Hasidic "misnagdim," literally meaning "opponents," were against the way the Hasidic yeshivas taught.

The founder of the misnagdim, also called the Lithuanian system, was Rabbi Elijah ben Shlomo Zalman (1720-1797.) He was also known as the Vilna Gaon. Gaon means "great genius in traditional Torah studies."

The misnagdim studied the Talmud profoundly. They asked questions and tried to find the deepest meaning of the rabbis' lessons. They wanted to figure out what the scholars in the Talmud *meant* to say. This was the way the Jewish faith studied the Talmud for thousands of years. Questions were encouraged, even questions about G-d. They always asked "why?"

The Hasidic way was not interested in wanting to know why. They believed blindly without question. They were interested in memorizing passages of the Talmud, that's all. They didn't study profoundly.

My father, a Hasidim himself, wanted me to study both practices. He wanted the Hasidic structure to give me the blind faith I needed, but for studying the Torah, Bible, and Talmud, he wanted me to get a deeper meaning. And my father had the power to make that happen.

In Baranovicze, there was only one of each type of yeshiva. He officially registered me in the Hasidic seminary, the Slonimer Rabbinical Seminary. But I considered the other seminary to be my primary yeshiva.

After a student registers at a yeshiva, the "rosh yeshiva," the dean of a rabbinical seminary, talks with the student to find out what he knows and what you've been taught to that point. Based on that discussion, he assigns a chavrusa to the student, someone you can study with.

The reason for this is to encourage discussion and therefore, learning. One student would ask a question and the other would answer, and together they would debate back and forth and learn even more together, than if they studied alone.

The Slonimer rosh yeshiva, Rabbi Samuel Hirshowitz, assigned his son, Yedidia, to me. Why he picked me, I don't know. Interestingly, Rabbi Hirshowitz was actually a misnaged. Maybe he sensed that I was not as Hasidic as my father, grandfather, and great-grandfather were. I'd already had exposure to the non-Hasidic Lithuanian system and understood the differences.

Yedidia was a rare and very funny person. He could not stand the Hasidic system. Like his father, he had a brilliant mind and always came up with creative ideas. He was a terrific person to be partnered with to study the Talmud in a profound way.

✶ ✶ ✶

My rabbi for the Lithuanian system was Elchonon Wasserman–his name was very important in those days. He was a tall, impressive-looking man.

Once a week, he used to walk from his home to the seminary to make a two hour speech—a lesson—to five hundred students. He walked slowly, taking his time, all the while thinking of something brilliant to say to the students. The Slonimer Yeshiva was on the same street as this misnagdim seminary and between his house and the seminary.

I would watch for Rabbi Wasserman from Slonimer and when I saw him walking up the street, I'd hurry out of the yeshiva to follow him. I did this because I knew he was going to lecture students after the walk and I wanted to make sure I heard his speech. Also I liked to observe him during his walk. He would keep his eyes down toward the sidewalk, hands clasped behind his back as he walked slowly lost in thought. I trailed Rabbi Wasserman with a lot of respect. I made sure to leave plenty of distance between us, so that I wouldn't disturb him. I don't know if he even realized that I was back there.

When he spoke, he was calm and cool; easy to understand. His speaking ability was a gift from G-d. It was as though he would put a beautiful meal on a plate—easy to visualize. His lessons became so clear. Plus he had a great gift for explaining things.

People called him "Tsung shel Gold," which is Yiddish for "Tongue of Gold." Students from all over, even the United States went there just to hear him. That's why they had a lot of students. There were heads of other yeshivas that gave similar speeches, but nobody, not locally or anywhere else, could match Wasserman's gift. Nobody.

He spoke in Yiddish, and his messages were so clear that you could not miss the meaning of it. I used to write it all down and sell his speeches to pay for my expenses.

Rabbi Hirshowitz at the Slonimer seminary, on the other hand, spoke very fast. He became so excited during his lectures that his face would turn red. He may have been even *more* brilliant than Wasserman, but there was a huge difference in their presentation styles. With Wasserman, you could memorize him. You could write his lessons down and always understand them in the intended way.

But with Rabbi Hirshowitz's machinegun delivery style, it was hard to catch what he was talking about. He was brilliant and had a fast mind, but he didn't know how to slow down and explain the lessons at an understandable pace. Sometimes he would interrupt himself with an entirely different or contradicting thought.

In time, over years of studying and listening to him, I became accustomed to his style of delivery. Eventually I was able to write down and sell his lectures as well.

People never spoke to Rabbi Wasserman, because they were afraid to talk to him. They were intimidated by his brilliance. Plus, he was not at the seminary every day.

Rabbi Hirshowitz, on the other hand, was at Slonimer Yeshiva every day and he was easy to approach. I spoke to Rabbi Hirshowitz often and asked him a lot of questions.

There were always great lessons to be learned from both rabbis.

My father covered my tuition, but unlike at Łomża, I didn't have a place to stay. I had to find a way to pay for food and rent! There was a time in the beginning, when I didn't have money to pay for the things I needed. So I slept in the back office of a bank, and acted as their security for the night.

The bank was a Jewish business that loaned Jewish people money with zero or very low interest. Big communities had these banks for the Jewish people.

They had set up a cot in the back office for me and another student, who stayed the night with me. In that bank was the only place in town where you could have access to a typewriter and make copies. I used their equipment to type up the lectures from the rabbis and then made copies, so that I could sell them.

I would mainly sell the lectures to other students, but sometimes the local people who came to our yeshiva to pray would buy them too.

Selling the lectures alone was not enough money for me to live on. One day when I was about fifteen years old, I went to the local barber and watched him work. Afterwards I bought a pair of manual clippers and began practicing on myself.

In a short time, without any formal training, I began clipping hair for everybody there. There were five hundred students! I was very busy, and sometimes a little *too* busy, but I made good money and was able to rent a real room, instead of staying at the bank. Plus I had money for food and other necessities. I could afford to wear nice clothing and live comfortably.

I was the only barber at the yeshiva. All the business came to me, and not only the other students, but also the teachers and all the elders of the town who prayed at the synagogue. My older customers always gave the best tips, since they weren't poor like most of the students.

In the seminary, on Saturdays, the students were supposed to read the Bible, the Torah Portion of the week, and continue their studies. I was renting a room near the yeshiva, so I wouldn't have far to go to take my lessons at the seminary every day.

But there were other options. There were some big homes with extra rooms for rent or properties where students could rent out an entire house. It was a house like this where a memorable story comes from.

There were three yeshiva students living in one house. On Saturday, the Sabbath, students didn't have to go to the yeshiva, they could rest, stay home, whatever.

One Sabbath, these students decided to stay home and play cards for money! The rosh yeshiva was taking a walk outside and passed by this house. He walked up and looked through the window to see what his students are up to. And lo and behold, he saw them sitting on the living room floor gambling on the Sabbath. That's a big sin!

The rabbi walked into the house and said, "What are you doing? It's Shabbat! You're gambling on Shabbat? What's the matter with you?" He turned to one student and asked him, "Why are you committing this sin?"

The student said, "I'm sorry, I didn't know that it was wrong."

The rabbi asked a second student the same question.

He said, "I forgot today was Saturday. I thought it was just a holiday."

The rabbi turned to the third student, "Okay, he forgot gambling was against the law, this one forgot today was Saturday . . . what did you forget?"

"Rabbi, I have to tell the truth . . . I forgot to pull down the window shades!"

Part II

Neutral Lithuania
(January 1940 – July 1941)

11

From Baranovicze, I took a long train trip north to Vilnius, Lithuania. When World War II broke out, and it was decided that Lithuania would remain a neutral territory, the Russians already had a presence in Vilnius. They agreed to withdraw their army from the city, as long as they could establish military bases in the region.

The Russians may have had their bases and some military personnel there, but the Communist system was not governed, so life was fairly normal. We were able to live a somewhat free and normal lifestyle.

We had access to good foods and other luxuries, but the Russians were still in control in terms of government. Lithuania couldn't do a thing to make agreements with other countries; Russia wouldn't let them. But Lithuania was under Russia's protection from Germany, and that was more important.

When I got to Vilnius, I tried to find out about my family, but none of the refugees who came to that shtetl knew of them. The newspapers did not discuss the details of what the Germans were doing with Jews they'd captured. The media kept it quiet or perhaps didn't even know the truth. The media before 1960 was very different from today.

I went to the big yeshiva in Vilnius and found most of the teachers and students from my Hasidic yeshiva there and some from the misnagdim yeshiva as well, including the great Rabbi Wasserman, whom I was so fond of in Baranovicze.

Some yeshivas were allowed to go to China from Lithuania with the help of the United States who had a presence in Shanghai. Some think that Russia allowed this because they would try to make spies out of these Jews to keep tabs on China or just to stay in good terms with the United States. Regardless, it's a little known fact that Jewish communities had developed in China.

Shortly after my arrival, the government didn't want us to remain in Vilnius, so they moved us to the other side of Lithunia, close to the German border. The shtetl we moved to was in the big city of Tavrig.

Only a small river separated us from the Nazis.

Once I got to Tavrig, I learned that thousands upon thousands of people were rushing to Kaunas, the temporary capital of Lithuania, looking for a way to get entry visas into countries away from the war. Since foreign embassies were present, there was hope that we would be able to obtain visas to get out of Europe and escape to the United States or Palestine.

Kaunas was about eighty miles east of Tavrig, so I went there too, in an attempt to get a visa. We had to wait in long lines outside the consulate—there were so many people with the same idea. During the lengthy application process, I stayed at the Slabodka Yeshiva, known as the mother of all yeshivas. Located only a few miles north of Kaunas on the other side of the river, the Slabodka Yeshiva was devoted to a high level of study of the Talmud.

When not standing in line, our lives consisted of studying the Talmud as though the war did not exist. I was fortunate enough to have been granted a visa to Curaçao, the Caribbean island north of Venezuela. I thought I would be able to get out, but the Russians, who controlled the borders, wouldn't honor the exit visa. They stopped me at the border.

They said, "No. You cannot get out."

They were only letting other Russians or those who agreed to be spies for Russia out of the country. They weren't letting the Jews or anyone else leave.

I was trapped in Lithuania.

I lived in Lithuania a couple of months before my twentieth birthday, March 25th, 1940, rolled around.

The Jewish holiday, Purim, fell one day earlier that year, on the 24th. Purim is a holy day, a joyous celebration of the survival of the Jews as told in the Book of Esther.

Purim *could* have been the first holocaust. This happened after the destruction of the first Holy Temple while the Jewish people were in exile in Babylon.

The king of Persia, King Ahasueraus, searched for a new wife to join his harem. He had killed his previous wife, Queen Vashti, after he became angry with her at a party, for refusing to present herself before his guests.

A beautiful Jewish woman by the name of Esther was brought to Ahasueraus by her cousin Mordecai, who urged her not to reveal her true heritage. Esther, in Hebrew, means "hidden." Ahasueraus fell in love with Esther caring for her more than the other women in his harem, so he made her his new queen.

King Ahaueraus's viceroy, Haman, was an evil man similar to Hitler. He made a law that everyone had to bow down to him. Esther's cousin, Mordecai, refused to obey this law. He did not believe in bowing down to false idols.

Haman was furious with him and wanted Mordecai killed, even prepared a certain tree with rope that only Mordecai was to be hung from. As if that were not enough, Haman plotted to wipe out the entire Jewish population, but he needed a reason for such genocide. He needed to persuade the king.

In Esther 3:8, he told the king, "There is a certain people scattered abroad and dispersed among the peoples in all the provinces of your realm. Their laws are different from those of every other people's, and they do not observe the king's laws; therefore it is not befitting the king to tolerate them."

This was enough to convince the king, so he gave Haman permission to deal with the Jews as he pleased. Before Haman could execute his plan to exterminate the Jews, Esther revealed her true heritage to the king. She made the king understand that if all Jews were to be killed under Haman's decree, then she would have to be killed as well.

This angered the king and he terminated Haman's decree. He ordered the execution of Haman; for him to be hung from the very noose meant for Mordecai.

Queen Esther had saved the Jewish people from extinction. Who would save us this time?

12

During the year and a half I was in Lithuania, from January 1940 to June 1941, it was like I was on a vacation from the war. We were there studying, living a fairly normal life for a year and a half. No bombings. No Germans.

The Russians were present just to observe the military bases, but they did not mix in. They did not interfere. Mainly, they controlled the borders; they were very good at controlling borders. Nobody could come in, nobody could go out.

Within the Lithuanian borders, we didn't even know what was going on in the war. The papers were forbidden to even write about it. Auschwitz had begun its ugly campaign and hundreds of thousands of Jews were being murdered throughout Europe, but we didn't know. We were isolated.

All of us yeshiva students were studying to become rabbis. The head of the rabbinical seminary knew that Germany was going to continue to conquer countries and that many rabbis were being killed. He felt it important to prepare as many of us as possible to become rabbis and to get us ordained so that there would be educated rabbis to teach the faithful.

To be truthful, we received it a little prematurely. Normally, we would've studied longer, but with the war, we did not have the time.

In Russia, it was a crime to be a rabbi or preach religion. In Lithuania, the Russians were starting to force their Communist beliefs on us, and it was now against the law for us to be religious. If caught breaking their laws, we could've been sent to Siberia. We had to live as practicing Jews in secrecy.

Considering the alternatives, we had a good life while living in Lithuania. I received my first "semicha," rabbinical ordination, during this time. It was signed by Rabbi Samuel

Hirshowitz, who was my rosh yeshiva at the Slonimer Yeshiva in Baranovicze.

Quite often, I thought about the conditions in Poland, and wondered how my family was doing. Were they even still alive?

There was not much talk about what was happening. Partly because the details were not getting to us, and the other part was that we were focused on studying profoundly to reach semicha.

Since we tried to keep our humor about things, occasionally a joke about the war would float around to break the serious mood. There was one about Hitler and his Minister of Propaganda, Joseph Goebbels.

Goebbels was one of Hitler's closest associates and most devout followers. He was held responsible for "Kristallnacht," the first organized attack on the Jewish people in Germany and Austria on the 9th and 10th of November 1938.

Before the Holocaust Goebbels told Hitler, "I don't think we should label the Jewish people as inferiors, because it doesn't make sense. They are actually very smart, because they have the Torah and the Bible—they're even smarter than the Germans."

Hitler couldn't believe his ears. He said, "What? The Jewish people are smarter than the Germans? Impossible!"

Goebbels said, "Let's go out on the street in the market and we'll see who's smarter; the Germans or the Jewish people."

They walked over to the market; there were both German and Jewish stores and businesses. First they went to a German store.

Goebbels said, "All right, let's see how good of a businessman he is."

Goebbels went up to the store's proprietor and said, "Can you sell me handled cups to be used for left-handed people? Can you sell me something like this? I'll need lots of them."

The businessman said, "What? Cups with handles for left-handed people? Very few people are lefties. I'm sorry, but I don't have any cups like that."

He said, "Okay. I understand." They left.

Goebbels said to Hitler, "He said he doesn't have any, yeah? You'll see. The Jewish people will have them."

They go into a Jewish store and Goebbels asks the owner the same thing.

The Jewish man says, *"Yes, we have them."* He takes a regular handled cup and puts the handle in Goebbels' left hand. *"There you go—a cup for a left-handed person."* He sold Goebbels the cup.

Hitler and Goebbels left the store. *"You see—who's smarter? The German owner couldn't figure out that the same cup can be used for both right* and *left-handed people!"*

13

During the spring of 1941, the Russians began to position tanks along the river and borders. We feared that an attack from Germany was imminent. Shortly after, the Lithuanian government moved us away from the border and relocated all the Jewish students to a small town called Shkudvil, approximately fourteen miles northeast of Tavrig. Over there, we had a big synagogue and school.

We weren't there for very long before another change would occur. With the threat of Germany invading, Russia occupied Vilnius again. They confiscated the records containing names of those who had registered for visas to leave the country. They believed that those expressing the desire to emigrate were opposed to Communism. Terrible news for us rabbinical students.

Our worst fears came true. There was an order by the "NKVD," the Soviet secret police, to round up all the yeshiva students, with the intention of sending those who had registered for visas, to Siberia.

Big transport trucks pulled up in front of our building one night. I was in my room and heard enough commotion from the secret police and my students in the hallway to realize they were coming to haul us all to Siberia. My heart pounded and I had to think fast. I had just enough time to jump out of my dormitory window before they reached my room. Once outside, I ran as fast as possible to a nearby cemetery.

A pair of NKVD officers were there waiting for me.

Again I had to use my wits, and in the hope that they only sought students who had registered for visas, I gave a fictitious name.

They scanned their list of names intently, multiple times, but did not find a match.

One of the policemen asked, "Why did you run away then?"

"I thought all the students were being sent away to Siberia," I replied.

"Next time, don't run from us or we'll take you anyway. You're free to go."

I realized, however, that someone would either report me or inadvertently reveal my name in conversation, so I ran back to the house where I had been staying. The owner of the house was a buggy driver named Tomof, who made a living with a horse and wagon. I was a good friend of his son and had been paying rent to stay there. Tomof hid me in the attic.

For weeks I stayed hidden up there, afraid to leave the security of the attic, while Tomof kept me fed. Most of the other students, a few hundred of them, had been carted off to Siberian slave-labor camps.

Tomof took a risk hiding me—he could have been sent to Siberia too, if caught. He was a good man and really helped me in those days. He had to close the door of the attic to keep me safe. I was up there alone in darkness and solitude with only my prayers for company. I only came down if I had to use the bathroom or bathe.

Mostly I read books or newspapers and studied during that period in the attic, but I also had plenty of time to think and reflect as well.

I worried a lot about my family, wondering what had become of my mother, sister, and young brothers. I prayed and prayed that they had found refuge from the horrors of the war. I reminisced about Rachel and how not long ago we were a young man and woman falling in love, and now I had no idea if she was even alive. And I tried to remember the good times with my father, but the images of his violent death kept creeping into my mind.

While in that attic I wrote a very emotional, sentimental song in Yiddish about the dark experiences I'd gone through; about the running, the fear, the suffering. I would cry big tears of sorrow every time I sang this song:

Dark is the night
And heaven is black
I'm lying in the attic thinking
And it hurts my heart
Will they invade again?
I'll be forced to run away
But my body still hurts
From when I fled the Nazis
The first time

14

By this point, we knew the Nazis were out to accomplish Adolf Hitler's Final Solution, a plan to methodically exterminate European Jews. But where did this hatred come from? And how was it able to happen?

The Nazi system was to systematically kill as many as they could until they got to the end. That was their goal. The Final Solution—to kill all the Jews.

The Germans, we don't know how many exactly, were sympathetic to Hitler mainly because he was a dictator. He didn't need the people's support or votes after he came into power.

They voted him in the first time, and once he was in office, he did whatever he wanted. Ten years before the war, in 1930, he was voted into power. Why did they vote for him?

Because Germany lost World War I, and had an economic crisis afterwards. There was the Great Inflation in the early 1920s followed by a Great Depression in the mid-1920s. The German middle class was ruined, and these events made it possible for Hitler to convince the people he could bring Germany back to prosperity.

Hitler started winning support by using hate. He pointed his finger and started to blame groups that he believed caused Germany to lose the war.

For some reason, he put the Jewish people right in the middle of it. Hitler would say that the Jews made them lose, because we were the investors and bankers, and we had profited from the war. He said the Jewish people became rich from Germany's defeat.

These were fictional stories, but a lot of German people believed them. Nobody wanted to admit that they had lost the war because they weren't good fighters. Many Germans learned these lies when they were little, and they grew up knowing no other truth. They blamed and hated the Jews for losing World War I. For them it was a fact, not a story.

There is a joke, probably based on a true encounter, but it has been passed down to prove a point.

There were two German soldiers walking down the street. They came across a Jewish man, so they grabbed him and began to beat him up. The soldiers asked him, "Who's to blame for us losing the war? Who made us lose?"

The Jewish man shrugged his shoulders. "I don't know."

"Tell us, the Jewish people caused us to lose the war. Say it or else."

"Okay, okay. The Jewish people caused us to lose the war ... the Jewish people and the pretzel maker."

One soldier said to the other, "What is he saying? The Jewish people, I know, I heard him say it. But the pretzel maker?"

The other soldier said, "What, are you kidding me? The pretzel maker? Why the pretzel maker?"

The Jewish man said, "Why the Jews?"

Maybe Hitler wasn't so crazy. There were millions and millions of Jews spread out through Europe. And plenty of them were wealthy and had riches, gold, jewelry, and valuable paintings. With this money, he could afford to fund his military. Germany was poor before World War II, so the Jewish wealth could keep him moving towards his goal of world domination.

How could he get all that wealth? He had to *take* it! Before he could do that, he had to kill or drive the Jews from their homes. He succeeded by conquering many countries, like Austria, Czechoslovakia, and Poland, and was able to retrieve the riches and continue to build up his army.

But the discrimination and hatred towards the Jews did not necessarily start with Hitler and the Nazis. Yes, Hitler and the German army were the ones attacking us, but they were only acting upon the thoughts that many other non-Jews had in Europe, including some of the Poles from my birth country.

Discrimination is something I knew and feared from an early age, before I knew of Hitler and the Nazis. It was something that each and every Jewish boy or Jewish girl had to face.

Long before the Holocaust, when I was a child, I was afraid to go to out in public outside the Jewish areas, as were all Jews. We were afraid to walk by certain Christian churches.

There were many good Polish people who were considerate and neighborly, but anti-Semitism and racism existed too. Some European Christians, like the anti-Semitic Poles around my shtetl, truly believed that the Jews were responsible for crucifying their Lord and Savior, Jesus Christ. That's why groups of them hated us, embarrassed us, and called us names.

They cursed us often—cursing the Jews was a common thing in those days. In Polish, they would call us "Dirty Jews." They'd scream, "Jews—go to Palestine!" We had to live with the discrimination and hatred—what were we going to do?

Where could we go to get away from this humiliation?

And it went beyond words. If we looked at these anti-Semitic Poles wrong or said something they didn't like hearing, they would threaten us and sometimes beat us up.

These things happened every day. Age did not matter. When I was a teenager, there were Polish teenagers who would threaten me and beat me up. Even at my yeshiva this treatment continued. I lived with my grandparents in Łomża and had to walk a mile or so through the city to school every day. When walking on the sidewalk, if Polish kids were coming towards me, I had to step down from the sidewalk on to the street and keep distance between us, because if they were anti-Semitic, they would've beaten me up.

The environment was already set for Hitler and the Nazis to come in and do horrific things to us. We didn't have anyone within our own country, outside of the Jewish community, to help save us. The anti-Semitic Poles believed that we deserved Hitler's wrath; they wanted it. Even though Germany invaded and took over their country and stripped them of their independence, at the same time they were happy with Hitler and the Nazis.

Why? Because he gave them homes for free. Homes of Jews that were now empty because his army had killed or removed their owners.

Hitler said, "Take it!"

Some of the Poles had big families, but small or no homes, so the Germans said, "Here—this is all yours!" These bribes helped win them over. These Poles helped out the Nazis by supplying them with information.

It wasn't only because the Germans gave them homes. Anti-Semitic Poles, like other European non-Jews with similar beliefs, hated the Jews because they believed our distant ancestors killed Jesus. Which was a lie; not true. But even if it were true, how can they think that is enough to justify the Holocaust? How can that be enough to justify attempting to wipe-out the entire Jewish population, to try to make us extinct?

As if making up the lie about Jews killing Christ wasn't enough, they used to say that we were drinking blood of children, blood of Polish Christian children! That we'd kill them and drink their blood.

How absurd! Our kosher traditions alone prove that could not be true. The worst thing a Jew can do is to eat meat containing any traces of blood.

The Bible says you are not supposed to eat blood. When you buy a piece of kosher meat, you have to put it in water for a half an hour, add in lots of salt and let it soak for an hour, then wash it off with fresh water, so the maximum amount of blood should come out. Then you can eat it. It's Jewish law.

Hatemongers even said we would kill Christian baby boys and girls and make our Passover matzos with their blood. How could they make such lies? How could reasonable people believe such lies?

Who used to start these rumors of us killing Christ and drinking the blood of Christian children? A handful of Christian priests and bishops with an agenda. That's who. Those few openly preached these falsehoods to their congregations! They claimed to be men of faith. Men of G-d.

Their Christian followers were blind enough to believe in the lies. This group of priests and bishops did this to kill and destroy the Jews. To hate is not enough if the Jews could survive.

But how could we survive the killing of 1.5 million children? They used to say that Jewish people would be punished one day for Christ's death. These religious leaders were responsible for the hatred, for creating the environment that made it possible for Hitler to attempt his Master Plan.

That's especially why I was afraid to walk by certain Christian churches to get to my destination. Anti-Semitism was strongest around these churches. If I had to get somewhere and I knew of a church like that would be in my path, I would find a way to go around it and stay out of their sight.

All that time in isolation in that attic was difficult. I had too much time to think about what was happening. How things would forever be different. It was a sad, sad time and I shed many tears.

I thought about my family, and the way things used to be, but could never be again. Our proud heritage would be tainted, and its continuation threatened. All that we strove for and built over the years, the generations, would be ruined.

15

On June 22, 1941, two weeks after I first hid in the attic from the Russians, the Germans broke their pact with Russia and began to invade Lithuania. They wanted to get into Russia, so the way to do that was through the Baltic countries.

Immediately, the Germans forced their way into the city of Tavrig, with little or no resistance from the Red Army.

Days later, while I was still in the attic, the German army and the Nazis came into Skhudvil. The buggy driver, Tomof, helped me escape by hiding me in the back of his wagon and covering me. I had nothing except basic clothing, a prayer book, and several religious articles.

Later I would learn that only a handful of Skhudvil Jews survived the occupation. The Nazis massacred almost every man, woman, and child in that town.

Rabbi Elchonon Wasserman was found and arrested in the temporary capital of Kaunas. He was murdered by the Nazis in Lithuania. His son, Simcha, escaped to Israel and survived the war.

Tomof drove me further east to another city, but the Germans were already there preparing to start another ghetto. He couldn't take me any further. He had a job and a family to tend to, so he had to go back, and I set out on foot once again.

I ran and ran from one place to another coming across occupied cities that showed signs of bombings, ruin and destruction, burned up synagogues, many, many atrocities.

During my walking, I came across three big pits. One was covered up well, another was half-filled, and the other one completely uncovered, piled with the dead bodies of Jews. Hundreds of bodies were tossed in each pit. The atrocity was eerily reminiscent of the pits I'd discovered in Tykocin.

Once again the distinct, foul stench of death stayed with me.

Walking around from place to place was exhausting, so whenever I could, I would jump on a train at night through an open door. If there were no open doors, I'd have to jump on the side of the car, hang on with one hand and unlatch the door's iron lever to get in. Anything to keep ahead of the Nazis.

I didn't always know where the trains were going, so sometimes I'd find out I was heading the wrong direction, and would have to jump off and wait for a train traveling the opposite way.

Finally, weeks later, I arrived at a well-known yeshiva. I thought if I found it I may be able to make some friends there, maybe I could stay. But they were all getting ready to leave already—it was no longer safe anywhere in Lithuania.

A small group of us left the yeshiva in search of a better place to stay. After a while, we came to a crossroads. In one direction was Vilnius and the other was Latvia.

I said, "I just came from Vilnius—it's not safe there."

"No, Vilnius is where we need to be."

"That's right," said another. "The others all went there, to the yeshiva."

"You're wrong," I insisted. "It's very dangerous there. There's too much movement with the Germans in that area."

The others would not listen to me. "Look—we're going to the yeshiva, are you coming or not?"

"No, I cannot go back there."

They turned and left for Vilnius.

I continued my journey alone and at one point I came across a small city that was occupied and showed signs of becoming a ghetto. There were maybe fifty or more Jewish men, women, and children piled along the street in a gutter with their throats slit from ear to ear.

I was frightened and wanted to get as far away from that sight as possible.

Before the war, 240,000 Jews lived in Lithuania. Of those, 220,000 were murdered by the Nazis and their collaborators. That scene of utterly senseless brutality will forever be embedded in my memory.

16

Around the Lithuanian-Latvian border, I joined thousands of fleeing refugees. The powerful German aircraft were soaring above, dropping bombs that were falling and detonating on all sides of us. It was terrifying. At any moment one might land right by me and it would all be over. I sprinted away as fast as I could while the ground shook from the deafening explosions and people screamed and ran all around me.

I literally ran most of the way through what was then Latvia, but my escape route was suddenly cut off when German planes dropped several thousand paratroopers on the road and land directly ahead.

I slowed down and looked around for an alternate passage when a large Russian motor car bearing a Communist officer came roaring up beside me. They also saw the doom that lay before us, so the officer ordered his driver cut through a dirt road in the adjacent forest.

Taking his cue, I followed the path he created.

Just inside the country of Latvia, I came to the Dvina River. It was a big river—too wide to swim. I had to wait for the boat that, for a few dollars, carried people to the other side. It was hard to get on this boat, because there were so many people from all over trying to get across the river, and the boat was fairly small. It was a long wait to get across.

I bypassed the long line, and when the full boat started off, I ran and leapt into the boat. Nobody stopped or questioned me. The ticket man was turned around collecting money from the passengers, so he didn't even see me enter and I didn't have to pay.

When I got to the other side, I walked up the river bank and fell on my face. I was beyond exhaustion. I slept right in that spot for a long time, for days, it seemed. Exactly how long, I don't know.

It was a long journey through Latvia to Russia, but I usually could find food to eat. Latvia was a small country with many farms, so I had to steal or beg for food, like I did in Poland, to satisfy my hunger and survive.

Sleep was difficult to come by since I was always afraid of getting caught alone. Sometimes I had to climb up in trees and try to sleep. With little rest over a long period of time, I grew weaker and weaker.

In the woods of Latvia, I encountered Russian partisans. This time, unlike the partisans I met in Poland, they were very well prepared. They were organized—they had communications. Some of them were somewhat anti-Semitic, but there were Jews mixed in with their organization as well.

They invited me to stay and fight if I wanted. But I didn't want to participate. By then, I knew exactly where I wanted to go and what direction to continue moving. While in Lithuania, we had maps that would occasionally post movements of the war for us. We'd already started thinking of where to run. My plan was to get to Russia as quickly as possible.

We all thought we'd have more time to plan our escape, but when the Nazis came into Lithuania, they came in with tanks and armored vehicles and from the sky with paratroopers. The Russian soldiers were scared to death. They gave in. Hundreds of thousands of Russian soldiers surrendered within days.

When I got close to the border of Russia, I met a rabbi. There were lots of rabbis in the area, but this one in particular invited me to his house where I stayed one day and one night so I could rest.

He was an old man with a long gray beard, but I never even got his name. When I left, he gave me a whole satchel filled with food.

Although I will never know the fate of that good soul, I will never forget his kindness.

Photo Section

Rabbi Samuel Cywiak's father, Rabbi Baruch Cywiak, teaching Hebrew to his students. Young Samuel is believed to be in the back row, second from the left. Photo courtesy of Israel Pshetitsky of the Wyszków Association in Israel.

Rabbi Baruch Cywiak (front row, second from left) on the board of directors of a Jewish bank. Photo courtesy of Israel Pshetitsky of the Wyszków Association in Israel.

The open market off of Rynek Street, the central street in Wyszków, that the Cywiaks lived off of. Photo courtesy of Howard Orenstein of the "Explore Your Jewish Heritage in Wyszków, Poland"

The long bridge over Bug River in Wyszków. This is the same bridge that Rabbi Samuel Cywiak and his father were forced across by Nazi soldiers during their death march. Photo courtesy of Israel Pshetitsky of the Wyszków Association in Israel.

The Wyszków bridge crossing over the Bug River. Photo courtesy of Howard Orenstein of the "Explore Your Jewish Heritage in Wyszków, Poland"

Photo of the great Rabbi Elchonon Wasserman, who Rabbi Cywiak studied under at the Lithuanian System while in Baranovicze.

The actual yellow star that was pinned to Rabbi Cywiak in the ghetto. In the center is "Jude," the German word for "Jew."

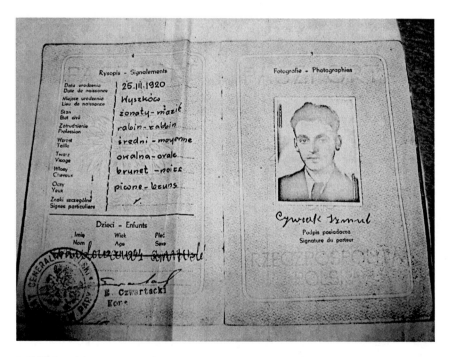

Rabbi Cywiak's passport that was granted after the war, so that he could travel to America.

RZECZPOSPOLITA POLSKA

URZĄD STANU CYWILNEGO w _Wyszkowie_ --------------

Województwo _ostrołęckie_ --------------------------

Odpis skrócony aktu urodzenia

1. Nazwisko _Cywjak_ -----------------------------------

2. Imię (imiona) _Szmul Benjamin_ ----------------------

3. Data urodzenia _dwudziestego piątego marca tysiąc_ _dziewięćset dwudziestego roku_ ------/25-03-1920/

4. Miejsce urodzenia _Wyszków_ -----------------------

5. Imię i nazwisko rodowe (ojca) _Chil Boruch Cywjak_ ---------

6. Imię i nazwisko rodowe (matki) _Rywka zd. Laska_ -----------

Poświadcza się zgodność powyższego odpisu z treścią aktu urodzenia Nr _48_ / _1920_

Miejsce na opłatę skarbową

Wyszków ---------------, data _1993-07-16._

KIEROWNIK
Urzędu Stanu Cywilnego

KIEROWNIK
URZĘDU STANU CYWILNEGO
w WYSZKOWIE

Chodkowska

Pu-M-8. zam. WA Olsztyn
Druk. ZP – »Spręcograf«

This Polish birth certificate had to be re-created once Rabbi Cywiak moved to America, in order for him to be eligible to receive a social security number. His previous birth certificate had been lost during the Holocaust.

YESHIVA UNIVERSITY
New York, NY

OFFICE OF THE DEAN OF MEN

January 20, 1947

Hon. American Consul
Paris, France

Re: Applicant Student
Szmul Cywjak
Paris, France

Honorable Sir,

Leading Rabbinic scholars, heads of European Seminaries, who are present in our country, have recommended that Szmul Cywjak be admitted to our Seminary.

The Committee on admissions has unanimously approved the recommendation of these Rabbis and has voted a scholarship which will provide for the student, tuition, room and board.

Our Seminary is the only one that has a college for liberal arts and sciences in connection with the theological training. Thus we are in a position to develop men theologically and secularly.

We most respectfully petition you, Honorable Sir, to grant a visa to the said student and make it possible for him to proceed to our country to pursue courses leading to the Rabbinate.

Respectfully yours,

(*signature*)
Samuel L. Sar
Dean of Men

(Above is a recreation of an original letter from the Yeshiva University of New York City to the American Consul of Paris, France, requesting a visa be granted to Rabbi Cywiak, so that he could attend the Yeshiva University on scholarship. Unfortunately, the original document was in poor condition and not printable.)

GLenville 1335-6

הישיבה הגדולה והקדושה דטעלז
קליוולאנד, אָהייא

Rabbinical College of Telshe
706-18 East 105th Street
Cleveland 8, Ohio

January 2, 1947

United States Consul
Paris, France

Sir:

    This is to certify that the application of
SAMUEL ZIVIAK to continue his studies in the
Rabbinical College of Telshe, Cleveland, Ohio,
...as been accepted for a period of three years.

    He will be provided with room, board and
full maintenance.

Rabbi Ch. M. Katz, Dean

SWORN TO before me and subscribed in my presence
this 3rd day of January, 1947

NOTARY PUBLIC

STATE OF OHIO)
CUYAHOGA COUNTY)

Rabbi Cywiak (left center) with his cousin, Rabbi Shlomo Goren (right center,) who was the Chief Rabbi of Israel for three terms.

HONE DICKENS 6-3354

RABBI B. NOTELEVITZ
1989 STRAUSS STREET
BROOKLYN, N. Y.

הרב חיים בן ציון נטולוביטש
רב ואב"ד דברוקלין, ניו יארק

RABBI OF
CONG. CHEVRA TORAH
ANSHEI RADISHROWITZ
139 AMBOY STREET
BROOKLYN N. Y.

With G-d help
Thursday of the portion Vayetze, 57720
[Corresponds to 10 December 1959]

I am the Rabbi and the head
of the Court of Brooklyn N.Y.

Here there comes before me the blessed and praiseworthy with great praises the Rabbi Shmuel son of Yechiel Baruch Cywiak, a light of Israel, Who has studied in the famous Yeshivot [Rabbinical Academies] in Lomza and Baranowitz, and who has studied with diligence Shas [Talmud] and Poskim [Rabbinic Authorities on Jewish Legal Questions].And he studied and was found, in accordance with the standards and the standards of the great scholars of his generation and they who were impressed by his intellectual capabilities. And the praised him and held him in high acclaim. And thus in my presence also, I proved him capable to serve foremost the realm of the holy and his loving esteem of the holy makes him suitable and prepared to perform as a Rabbi and to use Rabbinic Authority for he has great knowledge of the Shas [Talmud] and Poskim [Rabbinic Authorities on Jewish Legal Questions]. And all this he is hereby ordained as a Rabbi. And, beside his greatness in Torah and his stalwart faith in G-d, he is well-mannered and a person of good character. And, because he is a member and a follower of Talmid Chacham [a learned man]; he is worthy and capable to be a spiritual leader, standing at the head of a community. And, he is able to teach in the manner of our ancient Rabbis and to be held as a member of Talmid Chacham [a learned man] and of the great Yeshivot [Rabbinical Academies], and it is assured and indisputable that he will not do anything improper because of "Yoreh Yoreh" which affirms that he is empowered to rule on al questions of Halocho. And, besides the greatness in Torah, he speaks and teaches beautifully so that those who are instructed can benefit from his instruction and knowledge of the Torah. And, it is the desire of the holy Master of his power to influence the generation of our youth, to instruct them on the proper path.

Authored by one who honors the Torah and teaches it as a beacon to the righteous with the help of G-d.

/s/HaRav Chaim BenZion Notalevitz

/seal/Rabbi B. Notalevitz, Rabbi Chaim Ben Zion Notalevitz, Rabbi and Nobleman of Brooklyn, New York

I Rabbi Merrill Shapiro have translated this the letter, ordination certificate of Rabbi Samuel Cywiak by Rabbi B Notelevitz dated 10 December 1959 to best of my knowledge and ability.

Rabbi Merrill Shapiro

April 26, 2010

PHONE DICKENS 6-3354

RABBI B. NOTELEVITZ
1989 STRAUSS STREET
BROOKLYN, N. Y.

RABBI OF
CONG. CHEVRA TORAH
ANSHEI RADISHKOWITZ
139 AMBOY STREET
BROOKLYN N. Y.

הרב חיים בן ציון נטולוביטש
רב ואב"ד דברוקלין, ניו יארק

ב"ה [illegible] שנת תש[illegible]

הנה בא [illegible] המהולל בשבחות הרב ר' שמואל ב"ר יחיאל
ציוויאק נ"י תלמיד בישיבות המפורסמות בישיבת [illegible]
[illegible] ועוד [illegible]
[illegible] בש"ס ופוסקים. ועוד [illegible]
[illegible] הדבר [illegible] שהתחיל [illegible]
[illegible] נפתח גם [illegible]
[illegible] הקודש שיש לו [illegible]
[illegible] בש"ס ופוסקים [illegible]
[illegible] התורה. [illegible]
[illegible]
[illegible]
[illegible] דבר [illegible] גדולי הישיבות
[illegible] לתורה [illegible]
[illegible] הדבר [illegible]

הנני [illegible] כבוד התורה
[illegible] המצפה לישועת ה'
[illegible] חיים [illegible]
[illegible] נוטעלעוויטץ [illegible]

RABBI B. NOTELEVITZ
רב ואב"ד דברוקלין נוא יארק
BROOKLYN

B3

Here I with this [certificate] recognize the brilliant and highly respected Rabbi Shmuel the son of Yechiel Baruch Cywiak, Shalita [May he live days that are pleasant and long] who has appeared here as a Torah Scholar, G-d fearing and already ordained for teaching at the hands of the scholar Rabbi Chaim ben Tzion Notelevitz Shalita and it is right to depend upon him. This did well the important community of Caracas that is in the country Venezuela who received as a Rabbi and leader upon her and upon themselves. And it is upon them to honor and ennoble him as an expert Rabbi, luminescent and proud.

I set my signature on this on the day 5 Iyar 5723 [corresponds to April 29, 1963] in New York

Signed /s/ Moshe Feinstein

In the State of Florida, in the county of St. Johns, before me, the undersigned notary public, this day, personally, appeared Rabbi Merrill Shapiro who being duly sworn according to law, deposes the following:

I, Rabbi Merrill Shapiro certify that I am a bilingual translator, thoroughly familiar with English and Hebrew languages and that I have translated the attached document signed by Moshe Feinstein in New York on the 5th day of the Hebrew month of Iyar in the year 5723 to the best of my knowledge from Hebrew to English and the English text is an accurate and true translation of the a photostatic copy of the document presented to the best of my knowledge and belief.

_____
(Signature of Affiant)

Subscribed and sworn to before me this ___26th___ day of ___April___, 20_10_.

_____
Notary Public

מתיבתא תפארת ירושלים
MESIVTHA TIFERETH JERUSALEM
OF AMERICA

141-7 EAST BROADWAY
NEW YORK 2, N. Y.

Educating Our Youth ... Since 1907

WORTH 4-2830
WORTH 4-2832

[Handwritten letter in Hebrew]

B3

The Rabbinic Court for the Region of Jerusalem

Blessed is the L-rd Jerusalem May it be rebuilt and established. 21 Kislev 5723
(18.12.62) |Corresponds to December 18, 1962|

File 237/5723

The Honorable Rabbi, His honor, our Teacher, our Rabbi, Rabbi Samuel Cywiak Shalita |May he live days that are pleasant and long|,
Rabbi
in Caracas

Peace and Blessings |unto you|!

His letter from the second day of Parshat Vayishlach 5723 |Corresponds to December 10, 1962| we have properly received. And it is for us to make known through this |letter| that although it is known to the |Rabbinic| court in his place, there are factors impeding his delivery of the Get |Document effecting a Jewish Divorce| that we sent to him on the 18th of Cheshvan 5723 on behalf of the woman Esther the daughter of Benjamin (Mizrachi) who dwells in your city.

However, in the service of the honorable |Rabbinic| court, here we direct his honor not to attend at all to the impeding factors and only place before his eyes the issue of saving a woman from Agunah |abandonment by her husband| and remove all stumbling blocks and obstacles, it being forbidden to place stringencies on the wife of a man, and to deliver the Get discharging |her| with the full force our authority and also to include two others who honor their religion and are familiar with the sacred texts and to arrange the delivery into the hands in accordance with the laws of Moses and Israel and to send us confirmation of this by the hands of the representative.

And here we await his response and require it with all deliberate haste.

This to his honor the Rabbi with thanks from the start.

In accordance with the will of the The Rabbinic Court for the Region of Jerusalem.

The Chief Secretary,

/s/ |Illegible|
/seal/ The Rabbinic Court for the Region of Jerusalem
In the State of Florida, in the county of St. Johns, Before me, the undersigned notary public, this day, personally, appeared Rabbi Merrill Shapiro who being duly sworn according to law, deposes the following:

I, Rabbi Merrill Shapiro certify that I am a bilingual translator, thoroughly familiar with English and Hebrew languages and that I have translated the attached document signed by הַמַזכּיר הָרֹאשׁ on the 3rd day of the Hebrew month of Kislev in the year 5732 to the best of my knowledge from Hebrew to English and the English text is an accurate and true translation of the a photostatic copy of the document presented to the best of my knowledge and belief.

_____
(Signature of Affiant)

Subscribed and sworn to before me this 26th day of April ,
20 10 .
Notary Public

ביח הדין הרבני האזורי ירושלם   ת.ד. 1265.

ב"ח ירושלם ח"ו כ"א בסלו תשכ"ג.
(18.12.62)
תיק 237/חסכ"ג

כבוד
הרב כמוהר"ר סמואל ציביאק שלים"א
רב
בקאסאפראם

שלום וברכה!

מכתבו מיום ב' פ' וישלח תשכ"ג קבלנו אל נכון.
ויהננו להודיעו בזה כי אמנם נודע לביח הדין שבמקופי
ישנם גורמים שמעכבים בידו מלמסור את הגט ששלחנו לו
ביום י"ח חשון תשכ"ג עבור האשה אסתר בת בניבין(מזרחי)
מושבת עירכם.
אבל בפקודת כבוד בית ה ן הרונצ מצווים על כבודו
שלא יפנה כלל לגורמים המעכבי ורק לשיח נגד עיניו דבר
הצלת אשה מעגונה והסרת מכשול תקלה,אסור חמור של אשח איש,
ולמסור את הג"פ ליד האשה בנתעצת רשות מלאה מאתנו, אלא
מירצך עמג עוד פנים שהם שומר דת ויודעי ספר, ויסדר המסירה
ליד האשה כדמו"י, ולשלוח לנו אצור על כך מתום ע"י השלפם.

והננו מחכים לתשובתו החקובית בהקדם.

והננו בכנוד רב
ובחודה מראש,
במקדום _____ דושם

המזכיר הראשי ן

LOS NUEVOS GRANDES RABINOS DE ISRAEL

A newspaper article discussing "The New Chief Rabbis of Israel." Rabbi Samuel Cywiak (right) with older brother, Rabbi Label Cywiak (left) and cousin, Chief Rabbi of Israel, Rabbi Shlomo Goren (center.)

Only surviving photo of Malka Cywiak

קהלה קאראקאס ייִדישע הקהלה היהודית בקרקס

UNION ISRAELITA DE CARACAS

COMUNIDAD FUNDADA EN 1926

AV. CODAZZI No. 11, EDIF. MORAL Y LUCES, SAN BERNARDINO

TELEFONO: 544684   CARACAS - VENEZUELA   CABLES: "UNISCA"

Caracas, 7 de Agosto de 1962

CONSTANCIA

Por la presente certificamos que el Rabino

Samuel Cywiak

es el Jefe espiritual de nuestra Comunidad

en Caracas.

Natalio Glijansky
Director de Cultura

An official record by the director of culture stating: "I hereby certify that Rabbi Samuel Cywiak is the spiritual head of our community in Caracas."

מדינת ישראל
בית הדין הרבני האזורי בתל-אביב--יפו
שדרות דוד המלך 33 ת.ד.   טל. 21271

כ"ה, כ"א מנ"א תשכ"ד
(30.7.64)

מס' ‏282/64/65

תיק מס. 7964/תשכ"ד

לכבוד
הרה"ג הנעלה מוה"ר שמואל צביאק שליט"א,
קראקאס ווינירזואילא.

שלום רב!

הנדון: גט גליק-שרים

בג.ר. הזוג יעקב ואסתר גליק הסכימו ביניהם להתגרש. הבעל נמצא
כאן והאשה בקראקאס. לפי הידיעות שבידינו, שם האשה ואביה - אסתר
בת יעקב.

הרינו מבקשים מכב' לברר מפי הגב' גליק אם אמנם שמותיה
הם כנ"ל ואם אין לה שם נוסף, לועזי, שהיא משתמשת בו אולי בקראקאס.
כמו כן להודיע לנו שם שלאה

בתודתנו לחשובה בהקדם, הנני בכבוד רב

‏[signature]
סגן מנהל בתי הדין

The Adress:
Plaza Estrella
Edificio Astor Apart. 103
San Bernandino, Caracas

A document from the Chief Rabbinate of Tel Aviv Israel giving Rabbi Cywiak authority to perform Jewish divorces, and also refers to him as a "genius."

הבקהלה היהודית בבראאבם   יידישע קהילה קאראקאם

UNION ISRAELITA DE CARACAS
COMUNIDAD FUNDADA EN 1926

AVENIDA MARQUES DEL TORO, SAN BERNARDINO

TELEFONOS: 54 80 21 AL 25   CARACAS - VENEZUELA   CABLES: "UNISCA"

Caracas, October 28, 1966

TO WHOM IT MAY CONCERN

We have the pleasure to certify that Rabbi
Samuel Cywiak is, since July 1960, the spiritual leader of the Jewish Community represented by Union Israelita de Caracas.

David Katz
President

הקהלה היהודית בקראקם   יידישע קהילה קאראקאם

UNION ISRAELITA DE CARACAS
COMUNIDAD FUNDADA EN 1926
AVENIDA MARQUES DEL TORO, SAN BERNARDINO

TELEFONOS: 54 80 21 AL 25   CARACAS - VENEZUELA   CABLES: "UNISCA"

Caracas, Mayo de 1968

CIRCULAR Nº 12/68

Estimado Correligionario:

Con especial placer nos es grato invitar a Ud. y a su familia a la celebración de las

B O D A S   D E   P L A T A

de nuestro RABINO SAMUEL CYWIAK y su señora esposa.

El Rabino Cywiak sirve a nuestra comunidad desde hace 8 años y cumple su misión a cabalidad y plena satisfacción, y por consiguiente se ha ganado toda la simpatía y aprecio de la misma.

Esperamos que Ud., su distinguida familia y allegados nos acompañen en este acto de reconoci miento a nuestro apreciado Rabino Cywiak.

Aprovechamos la oportunidad para saludarle muy cordialmente.

POR LA JUNTA DIRECTIVA

Teodoro Fuhrman   Dr. León Wiesenfeld
Secretario General   Presidente

Favel Birnbaum
Director Asunt.Relig.

PD: El Coktail se efectuará en el Salón de Fiestas de la Unión Israelita de Caracas, el día Miércoles 29 de Mayo de 1968, a las 8.30 P.M.

An announcement that the Union Israelita de Caracas will be making a huge honorary party for Rabbi Cywiak and his wife for their silver anniversary.

unión israelita caracas

AVENIDA MARQUES DEL TORO, SAN BERNARDINO
CARACAS - VENEZUELA
TELEFONOS: 53.52.75 · 53.52.80

PYNCHAS BRENER
RABINO PRINCIPAL

הרב פינחס ברענער והרב שמואל צירוריאק מחייבים את עצמם
להלק ביניהם חצי את הכנסתם מאלה הדברים. ורק מאלה
הדברים, עד סוף חדש מנחם אב תשל'ב. ראלה הם הדברים:
חופה, תנאים. גט, ברית, מי שברר, לויה, אבלות. הקמת
מצבה, שלשים. גרות, פדיון הבן. השגחה.

An agreement between Rabbi Cywiak and Rabbi Brener stating that: "The Rabbi Pynchas Brener & Rabbi Samuel Cywiak obligated themselves to share between them 50/50 of all profits until the month "Av" May for the following: weddings, Brits, conversions, divorces, blessings, deaths, place of headstones, and 'Pidyon Ha'Ben,' (ceremony for redemption of the first born son.)"

(Der. a Iz.) José Weiss, Rab. Isaac Sananes. Rab. Samuel Ciwiak. El Ministro Andueza Palacios, Irwing Kriss y el Director de Cultos Dr. Rafael Enrique Briceño.

Rabbi Cywiak (right,center) receiving the second grade honor from ex-President Luis Herrera Campins.

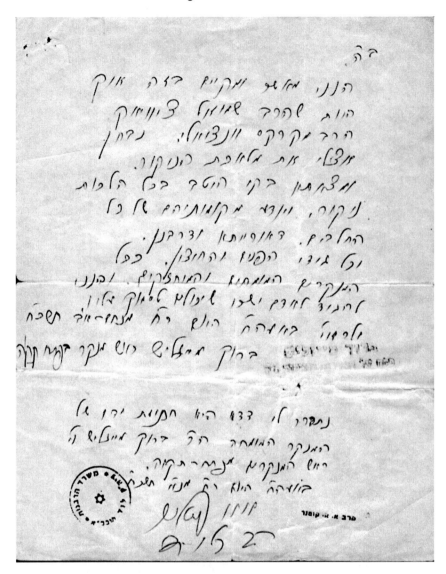

The Union Israelita de Caracas paid to have Rabbi Cywiak go to Israel to take a course on how to prepare animal buttocks so that the meat is kosher. The document above is from the Rabbinate stating that Rabbi Cywiak is certified in this process and authorized to train butchers how to properly clean this type of meat.

רבנות של ונזואלה
בית הכנסת הגדול של קרקס

RABINATO DE VENEZUELA
GRAN SINAGOGA DE CARACAS
Avenida Francisco Javier Ustáriz, San Bernardino
Teléfono 51-18-69 - Apartado de Correos No. 4.290
Cables: RABINATO
Caracas - Venezuela

Caracas,5 de Abril 1.973

Excelentisimo Señor Dr. Josef Shofman
Embajador de Israel en Venezuela
Ciudad.-

Excelentisimo Señor Embajador:

Tengo el honor de dirigirme a usted en mi condición de Presidente
del Rabinato de Venezuela para llevar a su conocimiento que el Rabino Samuel Cyviak es el Rabino Principal de la Gran Sinagoga de
Caracas,la cual es la Sinagoga del Rabinato de Venezuela;el Rabino
Isaac Sananes es Rabino Asistente del Rabino Cyviak en nuestra Sinagoga y el Rabino Dr. Yehuda Gartner es Rabino Ad-Honorem.

Aprovecho la oportunidad para enviarle mis más calurosos saludos
y deseos para el bienestar personal de usted y su apreciada señora esposa.

De usted muy atentamente.

Por el Rabinato de Venezuela

José Lerner
Presidente.

J.L/grl.

An announcement by Rabinato de Venezuela president, Jose Lerner, stating that
Rabbi Cywiak is the Chief Rabbi of their synagogue and has two assistant rabbis
appointed to him.

REPUBLICA DE VENEZUELA
MINISTERIO DE RELACIONES INTERIORES

ORDEN FRANCISCO DE MIRANDA

No._____

Caracas, 23 de julio de 1976.

167° y 118°

Ciudadano
Samuel Cywiak Lasko
Ciudad.-

Me complace comunicar a usted, que el ciudadano Presidente de la República, previo el cumplimiento de las formalidades legales y - por Resolución de este Despacho, ha tenido a bien conferirle la Condecoración de la Orden "Francisco de Miranda", en su Tercera Clase.

Al hacerle la participación que antecede, me es grato remitirle un ejemplar de la Gaceta Oficial donde aparece publicada la referida Resolución, el folleto contentivo de la Ley, y el Diploma correspondiente.-

Dios y Federación,

OCTAVIO LEPAGE,
Ministro de Relaciones Interiores.-

AJGL/sjt.
Anexo: lo indicado.

An announcement about Rabbi Cywiak being honored with the Francisco de Miranda order in the third class.

(Above) The ex-President of the Republic of Venezuela, Carlos Andres Perez, to decorate Rabbi Cywiak with the Francisco de Miranda order, as recognition to his efficacious activities to the community. (Below) A photo of Rabbi Cywiak wearing the Francisco de Miranda order.

CONGREGATION SONS OF ISRAEL
161 CORDOVA STREET
ST. AUGUSTINE, FL. 32084

Rabbi Samuel Cywiak,

Dear Rabbi,

It gives me great pleasure to inform you that at the Congregation meeting of

September 12, 2000, you were unanimously voted to a Lifetime contract as Rabbi

of the Congregation. This contract is in effect as long as you remain in good health

and able to perform your duties.

Mozel tov.

Sincerely yours,

Martin Broudy,
President

slf

First Congregation Sons of Israel
P.O. Box 352
St. Augustine, FL 32085

September 26, 2009

To whom it may concern:

I am pleased to write this letter on behalf of Rabbi Samuel Cywiak. He has served as the spiritual leader for First Congregation Sons of Israel for seventeen years since 1992. Further, because of his dedication to the membership of First Congregation Sons of Israel, he was presented with a lifetime contract from the synagogue by former congregation president Martin Broudy.

Rabbi Cywiak has been a practicing rabbi for more than 60 years providing spirituality to countless Jews for many generations. Moreover, he is a Hazan and a Mohel. Still further, he is a direct survivor of the Holocaust.

Our congregation is indeed fortunate to have a rabbi who is so eminently qualified to lead the congregation.

Sincerely,

Les Stern,
President

County recognizes Jewish History month

The St. Johns County Commission issued a proclamation on Jan. 12 recognizing Jewish History month. Rabbi Samuel Cywiak of Sons of Israel Congregation, the oldest congregation in St. Johns County; Rabbi Eliezer Ben-Yehuda of Beth El–The Beaches Synagogue in Ponte Vedra Beach; and Rabbi Mark Goldman of Temple Bet Yam were all present to hear Commissioner Karen Stern read the proclamation and present it to the three rabbis. The proclamation recognizes the contributions of the Jewish people to the settlement and development of St. Johns County and was issued in conjunction with the celebration of the 350th year of Jewish settlement in North America.

Article printed through the courtesy of The St. Augustine Record.

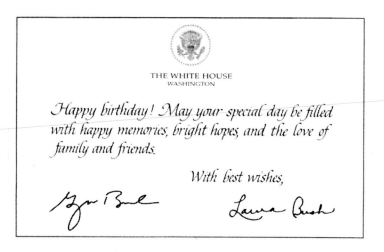

A birthday card from former U.S. President George W. Bush on Rabbi Cywiak's 85th birthday.

Rabbi Cywiak was presented this Certificate of Appreciation from Flagler College of St. Augustine for the many years of service he's provided by giving Holocaust lectures to the Flagler students at the Sons of Israel Synagogue.

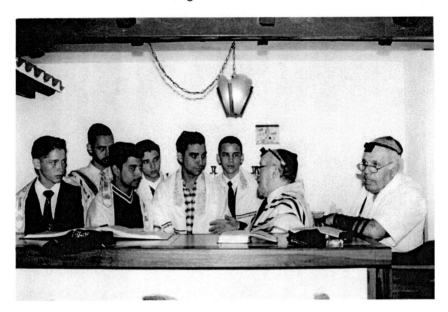

At a hotel in Colombia, Rabbi Cywiak forms a minion and wears phylacteries (on head and forearms) to perform a ceremony to convert a group of young men to Judaism.

In 2001, Rabbi Cywiak was given the honor of blessing the new building for the St. Augustine Record, the city's major newspaper.

Rabbi Cywiak hosting a luminary service in celebration of Hanukkah.

Rabbi Cywiak performing a wedding ceremony for his granddaughter, Sara.

Rabbi Cywiak's oldest child, son Chiam, pictured above with his two daughters (Susy on his left and Sara on his right) and their mother, Ahuva (far left.)

Rabbi Cywiak with his daughter Rebecca.

Rabbi's daughter Bernice with her granddaughter, Dana

Rabbi's youngest child, his son Baruch, with his family: Chiam's mother-in-law Fanny, wife Lya, son Mendy, daughter Carolina, Baruch, and oldest daughter Vanessa.

(From left to right): Bernice's daughters, Annette and Viviana, and Rebecca's daughters, Kyana and Cassandra.

Rabbi Cywiak with his six great-grandchildren (from left to right): Alan, Eilad, Jak, Dana, Stephie, and Jessi.

Rabbi and Mrs. Samuel Cywiak with the rabbi's commemorative plaque.
Contributed photo

Cywiak honored on 90th birthday

(Left) In 2010, the Flagler Hospital presented Rabbi Cywiak with a commemorative plaque for his service as a chaplain and for his 90th birthday. And article about this joyous occasion was published in the St. Augustine Record. The clipping is printed through the courtesy of The St. Augustine Record. (Right) Rabbi Samuel Cywiak with Rukmini, his wife of 32 years.

Part III

Communist Russia
(August 1941 – August 1945)

17

At the border, there were thousands of people waiting at the gates to get into Russia. Eventually they opened the borders and let everyone in at once. Just inside, a Russian railroad station had cattle trains lined up. We were piled into these cattle cars. It was uncomfortable, not only how tightly we were packed inside, but it was summertime and very warm.

The train headed further east, and inside one of these cattle cars I fell into a deep sleep. I woke in the morning and found nothing in my pockets. Nothing. Every document I had carried including my semicha, was gone.

I felt panic, but what could I do? I was robbed of everything, including my "tefillin," a pair of black boxes with leather straps that contain scrolls of parchment inscribed with Bible verses. The straps of the tefillin are wrapped around the arms and head during morning prayers. Why anyone would steal these is beyond me.

The only possession that remained in my pockets was my yellow star of David from the ghetto. It would remain the only item of mine to survive the Holocaust. I keep it with me in my pocket to this very day, as a reminder.

I still had the clothes on my back, but my shoes had been stolen, too. When I got off the train, I had to walk around in my stocking feet. I went a long time without shoes.

At one point, after traveling a while, we came to a big railroad station. I was a stranger in this country—I didn't know anything about it. I asked someone if he knew where my train was heading.

"You're going to Siberia to the Gulag labor camps," he said. "It's extremely cold and harsh. You'll work long hours in the ice and snow," he said. "It's almost certain death!"

I knew that the Russian soldiers would not let me walk off the train to avoid Siberia. If they knew I was a passenger, I would have to stay aboard until we arrived at our bleak destination. I came up with a plan. Before we arrived at the next station, I jumped off the train as it began to slow down, and rolled along the ground.

From there, I walked to the station and found another trusting face.

"Where do I go to register as a refugee?"

"You can do that at Gorki," the man said.

"Do you know how I can get to Gorki?"

"I believe a train is about to leave this station for that destination."

I needed to be on it, so I found the train and looked for an open door. When no one was looking, I jumped onboard.

I had to hide—I didn't have money to pay for a ticket. They also always asked for identification papers, and since I'd just arrived into the country, I didn't have any.

I had to be careful not to be caught at the station or trying to sneak into a railroad car, or they would put me on the next train to Siberia.

⊀ ⊀ ⊁

By the time I got to Gorki, Russia, the weather started to get very rough. The temperatures were freezing cold and snow and ice covered everything. My feet were frozen and it hurt to even walk.

I didn't find out what happened to my family until I got to Gorki. A lot of refugees came to Gorki—hundreds of thousands of us, not only from Europe, but also from Russia. Well, I met some other refugees there, who had heard of my family's name and knew what had happened to them.

"You're from Wyszków? Cywiak?" one of the men asked.

"Yes, my father was shot and killed in the woods by the Nazis, but I was able to escape. When I returned home, my mother, sister, and brothers were gone! I've searched *everywhere* for them, but have had no luck."

"I am familiar with your family. I have crossed their paths," he paused and sighed. "I'm sorry to be the bearer of bad news, but they were all captured in Łomża and sent to Auschwitz."

I was correct in going to Łomża, only I had arrived too late. My heart sunk. That glimmer of hope I held that they had found safety disappeared. Instead, my worst fears had come true. I wouldn't find out their exact fate until many, many years later. Mom, Nehama, and my three young brothers where all murdered in Auschwitz.

There was nothing I could do at that point—I was on the other side of Europe. It was too late for me to help.

I did not experience Auschwitz, but I came across this amazing poem that sums up some of the horrors that went on there:

AUSCHWITZ

Being in this place is very cold,
There are people of all ages,
young and old.
I don't even remember how I got here and why,
All I know is that I'm too scared
to cry.
The first thing they did was take
everything from us,
Then numbered us with tattoos to distinguish among us.
My mother, in Hebrew, is telling me to be strong,
But all I can think of is where's daddy, what is wrong?
They told us, if you do not work you will be dead,
I still don't know why but Rivka put down her shovel,
they shot her and I saw the blood pour from her head.
We're all hungry and determined to get out of here,
But nobody moves a muscle, I guess out of fear.
The days seem to pass, one into the other,
I wonder if he is still alive, my one and only brother.
Stories at night were told of different jobs that some were
forced to hold,
Sorting out possessions and clothes,
Removing the teeth that contained any gold.

Their skin used for lampshades, the fat used for soap,
In this hell on earth, there was no hope.
The surprise is not that so many died,
The true surprise is that any survived.
-- Erwin Kirshbaum

Erwin did not survive Auschwitz; she too was killed. But her poem survived to tell her story.

18

In Gorki, I went to the Russian immigration office where a serious-looking man asked me, "Who are you?"

"Well, I'm a refugee."

"Where were you born?"

"Poland."

"Where in Poland?"

"Wyszków."

He wrote it all down and registered me as a "Byezcyenyets," a refugee. The man handed me my "papers," my identification.

There were millions of people displaced from the war coming to Russia. Even some of their own people were without places to live. Many were being sent to Siberia to work hard labor outside in the frigid temperatures.

I was lucky—this immigration officer gave me an ID card with a job detail. I had permission to work a particular job—a "proper skill," they called it in Russia—and they arranged for my transportation, a combination of buses and trains that it took to get me there. This gave me protection from the cold weather conditions that were worsening every day, as we neared the winter months.

"You'll be working on a government farm in Shumarli. How many people do you have with you?"

Most refugees traveled with family—not too many people were like me, traveling alone—so I blurted out, "There are three of us. I have my family with me."

Without another question, the immigration worker handed me three tickets for travel on a nice, passenger train to Shumarli, Russia, as well as three ration cards to receive bread!

After leaving the immigration office, I headed for the marketplace. I approached a man, who I took for a fellow Jew, and asked him how I could find his rabbi. He didn't trust me at first, but I assured him that I was indeed a rabbi from Poland. He agreed to take me to see his rabbi.

I explained to the rabbi how I had escaped Poland, how all my belongings had been stolen from me, and that all I now possessed were three train tickets to a government farm in Shumarli.

"Oh, how lucky for you," said one of the rabbi's relatives. "In Russian, the name Shumarli can easily be changed to Tashkent."

Tashkent is the capital of Uzbeckistan—a Russian controlled country in the south—much further south, than Shumarli, which was north of Gorki in the heart of frigid Russia. Tashkent would be much warmer and desirable—exactly the break I needed.

They falsified my tickets, so I could travel to Tashkent. They did a perfect job on the tickets, and it was a normal passenger train too. I still desperately wanted to make my way to Palestine as my father had instructed me, but I couldn't do it alone.

The distance from Gorki to Tashkent was a long, long way. At least a week by train, covering thousands of miles with lots of stops. I had no money, so how was I going to eat?

I went to the marketplace again and found two willing Jews who would support me in exchange for the two extra train tickets; they were both yeshiva boys from Kaunas, the city in Lithuania where I tried to get an exit visa. Winter was fast approaching Gorki and the warm sunny region of Uzbeckistan sounded like paradise to them.

Before I left Gorki, the Rabbi gave me some money and a pair of shoes! He also provided a new pair of Tefillan, so I could fulfill my daily obligations as an observant Jew.

The agreement with my travel companions was that they had to feed me all the way until we got to Tashkent—that was more than a week of traveling. We bought food at every station. The farmers came to the stations and would sell vegetables, fruit, fresh baked bread, and other foods. They came right up to the train and we made the transactions through the windows.

After nearly two weeks of travel by train, my companions and I parted ways in Tashkent.

19

From Tashkent, I went by train to Ashkhabad, Turkmenistan, which was less than twenty miles north of the Afghan border. Since Turkmenistan was still within the Russian territories, I was free to travel there.

I was not free to travel to Afghanistan, which was outside of Russian control. The Russian military guarded the Russian-Afghan border very closely. But there were gaps in their patrols that could be taken advantage of.

One night, I tried to escape Russia by trying to sneak through the border. It was the middle of the night, so I thought I would have ample coverage. I crawled and crawled towards the fence. Before I could cut a hole and slip through, one of the Soviet guards grabbed me by the collar.

"Who are you? What are you doing here?"

"I want to go to Afghanistan."

"Why?"

"I'm a Byezcyenyets and I want to get to Palestine. Anything wrong?"

"Yes, there's something wrong. You're not supposed to go through the border like this. You're supposed to have your exit visa paperwork and go through border security like everyone else."

The problem was, they never gave out visas. They required us to have one to leave the country, but it was impossible to get hold of one. A situation that today would be called a Catch-22.

It was the same situation for people who wanted to enter the country as it was for those who wanted to leave. The Russians completely controlled the borders. They had millions of citizens, but they had a lot of soldiers guarding the border.

Pointing at my backpack, he said, "What do you got here? Take it off."

I removed it and handed it to him. He looked inside and found the black boxes of my tefillin. He opened the boxes and removed the parchment. He tried to read it, but could not, since it's in Hebrew.

He said, "What is this? It must be secret spy code. Oh boy, you better come to the office."

He called another guard over and they escorted me to the office, each guard holding one of my arms. In the office they started asking questions.

I told them, "This is used to pray. For my morning prayers."

"Pray? What are you talking about? You're lying. It looks to me like secret code. What is this language?"

"Hebrew."

"Yah, Hebrew, right! This must be secret code. And for that, you get," he said and drew his finger across his throat. During wartime, spies get executed in Russia.

I said, "Wait! Don't you have somebody who can read this? Can anyone here read Hebrew?"

The other guard said, "Yeah, maybe Boris can. Call in Boris."

Someone asked for Boris. A big Russian guard came in and took the parchment with the Hebrew written on it.

Boris looked me up and down, and then studied the parchments. Suddenly, he started laughing.

The other guard asked, "Why are you laughing?"

"No, no, nothing," Boris said as he looked me up and down again.

"There's nothing funny about this—this man has secret codes. He is a spy and must be dealt with!"

Boris began laughing again, this time harder. "What are you talking about? Spies? Codes? These are prayers!" He put the parchments back in the boxes. "This is tefillin. Jews pray with this every day."

"Huh? How do you know this?"

He looked me in the eyes and didn't respond right away. "My father used the exact same thing when he was alive. He was Jewish. He prayed with one of these every day, so let's forget about this. Let the man go."

I realized why he had been reluctant. In Russia it was against the law to practice religion, he could have been severely reprimanded for his admission. G-d Bless him. That Russian officer saved my life.

"Okay," one of the guards said, "we won't kill you. But we can't let you go through to Afghanistan either. We have a barge due to sail north to Nukus—we'll put you on that. There'll be work for you up there."

That barge ended up being full of Byezcyenyets; they were a brigade of painters. They all spoke Yiddish like me. They said they would teach me how to paint, so that I could have a trade and keep steady work.

The Russians had big houses built in Nukus, and we were to do all the painting there. A year's worth of work. It was slave labor.

We traveled way, way up, three hundred miles north to Nukus, a city with very few people. It was where the military worked near to the Caspian Sea, which is known for its caviar. Just outside of Nukus, caviar was shipped all over the world.

When we got there, we started working almost at once. I began to pick up the skills of painting fast. The first Saturday was a problem. I said, "I cannot work Saturdays. I'm a rabbi, and I must observe the Sabbath."

"What are we going to do with this guy?" They were worried because the Russians checked to make sure everybody showed up for work. They would do a line-up and a roll call. If I wasn't accounted for, I would be in trouble.

Someone came up with a plan. During roll call, when one of the Russian soldiers asked, "Is Cywiak there?"

"Yeah," someone would answer. And it worked!

We lived in a huge room with lots of beds. On Saturdays, I would get in my bed, and the others would cover me up with covers and blankets. And I would lie there the whole day. The cleaning people would come in, so I would stay still and quiet until they were gone. We made it hard for them to catch me.

All else aside, it was a fairly normal life in Russia; the Germans were far away, and I had a job and a place to live. The job paid very little, though, and the government ration card was only good for a small portion of bread. The big problem all throughout Russia was the food. The Russians had a major food shortage.

There weren't farms to steal from like there were in Poland. The Russian government had all the food packed up in large secure warehouses ready for deployment to be shipped to the big cities. Everything was government owned; the food, transportation, buildings, businesses . . . private-ownership did not exist.

We couldn't get sugar or salt. Even soap was hard to come by there. For food, all we could get was bread, and that was it. Every month, we would take our ration card to a government office to receive our bond for a month's worth of bread. To get the bread, we had to stand in a long line, sometimes a whole night just to get enough to survive on. If we lost our bond, or worse, our ration card, we could not collect our portion of bread. The whole system was government controlled.

We had to collect our rations of bread daily; maybe we could get enough for two days, but not more. The amount was so little that if we collected two days' worth of bread, we were so hungry we'd eat it in one day. The next day we had nothing, unless we could get something at the black market. We could buy food at the market with money, if we had any, or trade one of our possessions, like our belt, hat, or clothing for food.

One day after standing in line for hours, a Russian soldier approached me. During this time in the war, some of the injured soldiers had returned to town and needed to wait for their bread ration just like everyone else.

"Dirty Jew!" he yelled and pushed me to the ground. I looked up to see that he stole my position in line.

I stood and brushed myself off. "Why did you do that?" I asked.

"Why? Because you're a dirty Jew! Here you are getting free handouts while good Russians are getting shot and killed, fighting your war! Makes me sick!"

"It's not my fault."

"Yes it is!" The soldier lashed out and assaulted me with punches and kicks. I covered up to protect myself as best I could until he stopped.

"Why are you *attacking* me?" I asked.

At this point, we were beginning to attract attention. Just because he was a Russian soldier, didn't mean he was safe from the NKVD, the Russian secret police. They were everywhere and spied on everyone, including their own military. We had to be careful, because they could be posing as Russian civilians. There was a saying, any time two people were having a conversation, a third person was always involved, to spy on them and report the discussion to his superiors.

"Because you screamed at me!" the Russian soldier hollered for everyone to hear. Even though I did no such thing, this was his excuse so that he wouldn't get into trouble.

I had no choice at this point, but to retreat to the back of the line.

Here I was away from the Nazis, yet the discrimination only continued. Incidents like this would reoccur time and time again, to me and other Jews, while we waited in the bread lines.

I stayed at the worksite in Nukus for about a month. Hiding every Sabbath started to become dangerous. It was a tremendous risk. *This can't go on for very long. I'll be caught and sent to Siberia, or killed*, I thought.

Not wanting to take that chance, I ran away to the docks and I jumped onto a barge, which took me back to the cities in Uzbekistan.

20

I made my way southeast to the city of Bukhara, Uzbekistan. Thousands of Jews were living there. Some of the local Jews were believed to be ancestors of the "Lost Ten Tribes," ten of the original twelve Hebrew tribes who created the northern Kingdom of Israel.

The Jews in Bukhara had a very religious life with a nice synagogue. Now that Russia was at war with Germany and allies with America, these people were left alone.

America had urged the Russians to let the Jews out of Siberia, so they could have a chance to survive. Now there were thousands of refugees from Eastern Europe and Siberia living in Bukhara.

In Bukhara, I was sent to work picking cotton from fields for twelve hours a day. The Russians who ran the plant gave us nothing, except soup and bread. We could practically swim in the soup—there was nothing to it. It tasted horrible and didn't even begin to satisfy our hunger. That's all we ever had to eat.

The living conditions were no better. All the workers lived in one big room with a lot of straw spread around. The beds were dirty and made of straw mattresses that contained bed bugs and lice.

During winter time, I came down with typhus and became terribly ill. A group of us were infected, not just me. We contracted it from the insects in the mattresses. They took twelve of us to a hospital next to a big city.

The hospital staff used to leave us a piece of bread on our cushion, so we had something to eat. If I fell asleep before I ate mine, it would be gone when I woke up. Some of the other patients who had a little strength ate their portion, and maybe mine as well, but I didn't get any. When I felt a little stronger, I complained to the staff, so they brought me more bread.

Once I healed, I had to leave the hospital and go back to that infested straw! I was so weak—where else could I go? From the hospital, which normally took an hour or two to walk, it took me all day to get back. I could only take one feeble step after another. I didn't even have a walking stick to help me on my journey.

I passed by little Uzbeki villages and at one point came across a group of children. They were traveling along with mules and singing an Uzbekish song, one that I heard children singing all the time.

They stopped singing and came toward me hollering, "Who is that?"

A boy nine or ten years old came up to me and began taunting. I wore a belt over my coat to hold it in place. He stole my belt and ran away singing all along. He was just a young boy and I couldn't do a thing. I was so frail that I could not resist or fight to get it back. That boy's face has always stayed with me.

What could I do at that point but walk? I walked and walked and finally got there. I found out that only two others besides me survived the typhus. I remember one devastated boy sat on a bed crying. His father had been one of the victims.

The next day, I went back to work picking cotton for a few days a week. And little by little I got stronger. I said to myself, *Is this going to be my life forever?*

After working a while longer with these terrible living conditions, I contracted malaria. I would feel terrible with fever and alternate between breaking out in a cold sweat and having the chills. I didn't want to go back to the hospital where I was sure to die and I couldn't stay on that plantation any longer.

One night I snuck away and left for good.

21

From Bukhara, I went to the big city of Andizhan, also in Uzbekistan. It was now the beginning of 1943, when the Russians began their offensive against the Germans in Stalingrad. I'd been in Russia over a year already.

I found a black market, and traded my hat for something to eat and drink. I got a piece of round bread. I had to eat it plain since there was no butter or jam. There was no coffee or tea available, just a beverage that was basically hot water and contained no flavor. I needed something to drink with my bread, so I got some. They had milk too, but it was expensive and I couldn't afford it.

The black market was not only perfectly legal, but completely necessary; otherwise, people would die of hunger. Even if we didn't even have money, we could still exchange a hat or belt for a bit of food.

I stayed there eating and drinking, and somebody approached me. I looked at him and he looked at me.

"Moishe?"

"Shmuel! That's you?"

Moishe Tryzmel was a friend and fellow student of mine from my shtetl of Wyszków.

"Yes, yes—it's me. Just a little thinner than you remember. I can't believe it's really you, Moishe."

He was thin too, but he was a very tall guy, so he usually looked thin anyway.

We laughed and came together in a big embrace. The joy of seeing someone who was a dear friend, out here far, far away from our shtetl was more than I could ask G-d for.

He took me to his home where I was fed. Potatoes, soup, bread, and milk; more than I'd eaten in a long time. I slept like a baby that night. I finally had a good place to stay, with a good friend and his family, which consisted of his mother and two sisters.

The next day we sat around talking, catching up. I told him all about my journey. He felt terrible about my family, but was happy that I had survived so many close calls.

"So tell me, Moishe, how did you end up here?" I asked.

"When the Germans started bombing Wyszków, we ran for the woods. Me, my parents, and my sisters. From there we kept running, never looking back, and slowly worked our way into Russia."

They had made it to Minsk and began working long, hard hours every day under the Russian government. They couldn't even make enough money to purchase basic food or clothing. They didn't know what to do.

Just then the Russians announced that all who desired to leave for the United States need only register for visas. Not realizing that this was a Russian trick to weed out those dissatisfied with Communist rule, nearly the entire population, including Moishe's family, registered.

That night the NKVD rounded up all who had registered and sent them off to Siberia. His family was packed into a truck with about fifty others for the two and a half week trip to Siberia. The only food they received on the trip—during which the NKVD men kept guns pointed at them to discourage any escape attempts—was when the truck passed through large centers of population. This act of "kindness" was so the residents could be fooled into thinking that the prisoners were being treated well.

They arrived at Pucholek Uchfosh, and were immediately told that those who could work would receive food. Those too old would not.

The barracks were constructed of thin wood, no barrier against the intense Siberian cold. The inmates had no beds, and instead, slept on boards.

The menu did not vary. For every meal was a small piece of black bread and some foul-tasting, watery soup.

As lumberjacks, Moishe and his family worked six days a week for ten hours each day chopping down trees. The temperatures would drop to thirty-two degrees below zero. They and the rest of the slave laborers did not want to stop working in the coldest weather, for fear of freezing to death if they were not active.

The severe conditions were harsh on his parents, and they could not continue working after a while. Since persons who were too old to work could not receive rations, Moishe and his sisters would smuggle portions of their meager rations in their shoes to give to their parents.

Moishe's older sister Malka was caught doing this one day, and the Russians threatened to kill her, but spared her when urged to do so by the rest of the inmates, who liked her.

Soon afterward, Moishe's father, who I knew very well in Wyszków, went back to work and froze to death cutting trees. People froze to death all the time in Siberia.

Malka ended up with frost bite covering an entire leg. She could still walk on it, but her nerves were permanently damaged.

In 1942, a pact the United States, Great Britain, and Poland made with Russia to destroy their common enemy, stipulated that all Polish refugees in Russian slave labor camps should be freed. Once the war was over, Russia would have to help return them to their homelands.

Once released, Moishe and his family ended up in Andizhan only months before I met up with him.

22

A short time later, I started looking for work. I found a job painting inside of a government bakery. While painting, I was eating. I grabbed bread and ate until I was completely full up.

Once content, I would start putting bread pieces into my pockets. When I got home, I'd take off my clothes and bread would fall all over the place. Moishe's whole family would rush over and grab chunks of bread.

Sometimes I would take a chance and bring home a whole loaf or even a cake. I had these big buckets I used to mix my paint for the day. By the end of the day, the paint would be used up and the bucket would be empty. If the opportunity presented itself, I'd wrap up a full loaf of bread and put it inside the bucket and hook the bucket to the end of a long-handled paint brush. I'd carry the pole over my shoulder with the bucket dangling behind me. Even though everyone knew I was a painter, it was still a big risk in the event I got caught.

When coming and going from the government areas, there were gates with guards. If a guard stood in my way, I would walk straight at him with the top of the long-handled paint brush aimed at his head. I acted like I didn't even see him. It never failed. He would always jump to the side and out of my way. He wouldn't even have a chance to look in the bucket!

We settled for eating the pieces I had in my pocket, so I could take the loaf to the black market to sell for other things we needed to help us survive.

I searched for extra work that would gain me access to other foods I could bring home. That's what everybody tried to do to survive—

steal something. We didn't get much from the jobs, so we had to rob. Working hard didn't translate to anything more; everyone got the same low wages and ration card for the government provided bread. That little brick-sized chunk of bread was supposed to last us the day? Ridiculous! The government bakers used lots of water to make the bread in order to make it cheap and have the ingredients last longer. With all the water they used to make the bread, it wasn't dense enough to fill anyone up. It was terrible; light and moist, like eating nothing.

The wages were so low we couldn't buy much with it, because the value of their currency was so bad, especially with the war effort. We couldn't buy anything at the black market with the wages we earned.

To survive, we had to rob and steal from the Russian government, which was everywhere. The shops, businesses, everything, belonged to the government.

This was why the bakers made the bread with so much water, so they would have ingredients left over at the end of the day to sell on the black market.

If someone worked as a painter, like I did, he had to steal the material used to make the paint. This had a value on the black market too. When I could, I'd steal the material straight from the government warehouse where all the paint materials were stored. I would put the stolen paint in my mixing bucket, cover it, and sell it to buy food, usually some bread or butter.

Everybody had to do these things or die from starvation.

23

One day Moishe and his family started to talk to me about marrying Malka, the older of his two sisters. I felt that it would be a positive arrangement. I had been running long enough on my own; it was time to have somebody special to go on this journey with.

It would also be nice to have a woman's touch in my life. I was a typical hardworking man, doing physical labor, and a wife would help to make sure I kept clean by helping me to maintain proper hygiene and washing my clothes. Not that I had very many clothes, but it was good to have clean clothing from one day to another . . . even once a week was better than nothing. Plus, if I had a woman to keep me clean and keep things tidy, I wouldn't contract more diseases, so I would have a better chance to survive.

In Russia, people with families had a better chance of survival than those who were by themselves.

When I was alone and on the run, and I got dirty from work or traveling, I'd have to wash my clothes every so often in a river or pond. It's not easy. And then I'd have to dry them out in the sun, hang them on tree branches, or stretch them out on rocks while I waited around naked.

But if I lived in a house, with a family, I'd get to have a more normal life. I was tired from all the running. I thought it would be a good idea for me to have a family, so I agreed to marry Malka.

I would still get the shakes through my entire body, especially in my hands, from the malaria. Leading up to my wedding, I used to get attacks every day and had to take an herb called Cinchona that would help with the symptoms. It was a black bark that I would mix into water. The taste was bitter, but it was the only relief I could get from malaria.

On the Jewish holiday of Purim, in 1943, the Polish counsel arranged for Rabbi Lifshitz to officiate my wedding to Malka. Our wedding day was also my birthday and I turned twenty-three. It was a small affair though, just family and several friends. We were barely able to form a "minyan," a group of ten Jewish adults required for some of our religious duties. A Jewish wedding does not require a minyan to be present, but it makes it more official.

Our wedding clothes were very plain—we didn't have access to any type of formalwear. We couldn't afford elaborate decorations or food. We barely had enough food to survive on a daily basis, but Malka was able to get a little extra food from her new job at the Polish consulate to help with our celebration.

The most special and sacred part of a Jewish wedding is the Seven Blessings recited by the rabbi. Years later, when I became chief Rabbi in Caracas, Venezuela, I started a trend where I would sing these blessings when I performed weddings. It became very popular—people loved it. Other rabbis began to sing them too!

On the night of my wedding, Malka and I went to bed as husband and wife, and when I woke up the next morning after our marriage, the malaria was gone.

It was a miracle!

Over the years, I have asked a few doctors, and none of them had an explanation for this healing. Malaria is supposed to stay with you your whole life, but from that morning on, I've never had another symptom.

24

Weddings and birthdays aside, Purim has always been a special time of the year for a Jew. Esther spared her Jewish people from extinction, and prevented what would have been the first holocaust.

I have often wondered—*could* the Holocaust have been prevented this time? Was there sufficient warning? Was it predicted in the Torah?

I believe that the Torah *did* predict that there would be the return of someone like Haman who would want to wipe out the Jews.

The history tells us that hundreds and hundreds of years before Purim even occurred, the pagans complained to G-d.

"Why don't we have a Moses like the Jews have? What do you want from us?"

The pagans believed in everything, not one G-d. They didn't want something they couldn't control or see; everybody wanted his own god or many gods. The father of Abraham was a preacher and made statues. The pagans would buy the statues and worship them.

There were many natural disasters in those days like earthquakes, tsunamis, and typhoons. The pagans didn't understand those natural disasters, so they sought protection. They were desperate; holding on to anything they could for hope. They didn't feel the spirit of G-d. They didn't believe in a certain presence in the world, one who creates everything, cares for everything.

The pagans accepted any natural disaster as a punishment from G-d. They used to pray and complain to G-d.

"G-d, why are you punishing us? Because we are bad? The Jewish people are better because they have a Moses—we do not have a Moses."

"Who do you want for your Moses?" G-d asked them.

They selected a Gentile named Balaam. G-d appeared to Balaam and gave him a gift. Balaam became the pagan prophet and could foresee things that the other pagans could not. He became very famous, because he was like the Moses of the Pagans.

Balak, the king of Moab, made Balaam his personal prophet. Since Balaam received visions from G-d, the king had to listen to him. He didn't speak to G-d as Moses did. G-d communicated to Balaam through dreams and chance. The idea was for Balaam to teach the pagans to be better people. And he tried to do this.

The Jewish people were Balek's enemies. He wanted to kill them all, but he couldn't because G-d guided the Jewish people out of danger and eventually led them to Israel.

On their way to Israel, the Jews stopped in the mountains to rest. Watching from afar, the king told Balaam, "Look, I cannot fight these people—they have G-d's help and they always win. What can we do? Give me an idea."

"Well, it's very hard to go against G-d. If he wants them to win, they'll win."

"Can you, as a prophet, curse them? This way we'll get rid of them without military actions."

Balaam said, "How much you going to pay me?"

"I'll give you as much as you want."

Balaam rode on a donkey and wagon into the desert to approach the Jewish people in the mountains. First G-d sent an angel who stopped the donkey. The animal started talking to Balaam.

The donkey said, "What do you want me to do? Here's an angel sent from G-d, so I cannot go on."

Balaam realized that G-d would interfere and didn't want him to proceed with his plan. G-d gave this warning, but let Balaam go.

Balaam continued up into the mountains while the Jewish people were in the valley below. He got out of the wagon and looked down planning to curse them. G-d made him say just the opposite of what he planned to say. Instead of cursing them,

Balaam started blessing them. (That blessing is something we read every Friday night.)

Balaam realized how nice and beautiful the Jewish people seemed. He couldn't see any reason to have them killed. Even the way the tents were setup were impressive. G-d had told Moses to have his people make their tents so they should not look into one another; there should be privacy. Balaam was very impressed, because the pagans didn't put importance on things like this. When Balaam saw all the beauty of their lifestyle, he couldn't help but to bless them.

Later on, Balaam went away and reported to the king. Balak was furious with him. On his way back to his house, Balaam got a shocking vision and he told it to the people.

The passage in the Torah that contains this vision is noted as "an obscure verse." Their translation: "And he took up his parable, and said, 'Alas, who shall live after G-d hath appointed him?'"

Who is the "him" being referred to in this passage? It's a mystery. The Torah scholars interpreted the passages as such: *To survive the terrible catastrophes throughout Israel by Syria. Appointed by G-d to be the wrath of his anger.*

Long after this event with Balaam occurred, the Syrian Greeks overtook Israel and destroyed the first temple. The translators decided that this obscure verse had to do with the destruction the Greeks brought to the temple.

This explanation doesn't even make sense. I can't accept it.

From Hebrew, the first word should not have been translated as "Alas." The translation should have been "Oy!" as in "Oy vey," a Jewish expression of woe or exasperation. This is the only passage in the entire Torah where the expression of "Oy!" is used.

The use of that expression when this prophecy came to Balaam shows us that he was shocked by it. This prophecy *had* to have had a serious meaning; he discovered something terrible from it.

I don't believe that the balance of the translation from Hebrew is accurate. "Alas, who shall live after G-d hath appointed him?" has no real meaning. I've studied the Hebrew and there is an actual name in the Torah, instead of "him."

My interpretation would read like this. "Oy! Who is going to survive the name of Alef Lamed?" Alef translates to Adolf and Lamed means the son of Lisa. Lisa was the name of Hitler's mother. This passage has to be referring to Adolf Hitler.

Of course, I can look back and interpret this verse knowing what happened in our history. The scholar's interpretations were done long before the Holocaust, so how could they have known or interpreted it that way? The true interpretation did not make sense to them! Even if they did translate it into the correct words, who knew what "Alef Lamed" meant? They needed something that could be understandable, but even with their translation it was still marked as "an obscure verse."

Only a survivor and scholar, like me, can see the truth. I've discussed my interpretation with other scholars and they agree that it's the only thing that makes sense.

The Holocaust has resolved this mystery.

Although the Jewish people have had our share of tragedies, nothing in our history can compare with the Holocaust.

We should have a worldwide population of billions of people, because we are the oldest people in the history of mankind. Abraham was alive over four thousand years ago. The Jews should have the biggest population in the world!

But we were thrown out of Israel and spread out all over the world. Millions of Jews disappeared by being killed or assimilated.

The Christian belief took over a large percentage of Jewish people. Over five hundred years ago during the Spanish Inquisition, millions of Jews were driven out and destroyed. Our numbers have been cut down and cut down, largely through assimilation.

Our population has been stunted over centuries of events. We had no homeland, but we were still a strong, spiritual people, because it is not possible to wipeout an entire people.

Adolf Hitler thought he could. He killed over six million Jewish people in a short time; no one else in history came close to doing that. He was the only one. That's why the Holocaust is the greatest tragedy in the Jewish history, and probably the greatest tragedy in the entire history of mankind.

What are we after all this tragedy? Approximately six million Jews are in Jerusalem. Another six million in the United States. The rest of us are scattered across the rest of the world. There are only between 15-20 million Jewish people worldwide.

We almost disappeared.

So when Balaam asked, "Oy! Who is going to survive the name of Alef Lamed?"

He saw the horrors that waited for us.

25

Just before our wedding, Malka got a job working for the Polish consulate in Andizhan, Russia. With that job came some additional privileges.

Malka and her co-workers would get extra bread and even rare food like a cut of meat. Normally, you could not find meat anywhere. If they did have any at the market, it would be far more expensive than we could afford. I didn't eat meat because it was not kosher, but it was good to have some for the others.

I still worked as a painter for a government company. I would get the bread rations and materials to paint with from the government and use the extra material, or materials I took from the warehouse, to paint private houses on the side. The owners used to give me rice or wheat to make bread. I didn't want money; I wanted decent food for my family. The side jobs became very profitable for me. I would receive goods that I could either use or sell.

The side jobs that I found in the country were even better, because they gave me rice, potatoes, tomatoes, and even meal to make bread. I sold any surplus on the black market for bread, butter, and sugar.

This was our way of life under the Communist system, what we had to do to survive. We were waiting for the war to end, so that we could go back to our homeland.

Not once did we think about settling down and staying in Russia, because we couldn't live like thieves forever. That was not a life that we knew from Poland. We didn't have to *steal* in Poland. It never dawned on me before the day my father was murdered I would have to steal some day to survive! We were raised to live good, honest lives, and *not* steal. In Russia, we had no choice but to steal.

I know that G-d forgave us for doing so.

The war was nearing the end. The Soviets were pushing the Germans back towards Berlin. We were located in a place where there were no bombs, no shootings. It was far away from the war.

But danger still existed; there was the Communist government to worry about.

One day a wave of fear engulfed Andizhan, as hundreds of men and teenage boys mysteriously disappeared without a trace. Husbands left their wives for work and students left their homes for school in the morning, and like a scene in a horror story, they were never heard from again.

The Russians were constructing a new canal in the vicinity. It was an enormous job, and very physical and demanding work. Deaths from disease and malnutrition were numerous among the workers who lived in the filthy conditions provided by the Soviet government.

It soon became evident that the secret abductions of these men and boys were to force them to work on this monstrous canal project. Work that almost guaranteed death.

One night I was coming home after a long day's work and was grabbed by a couple NKVD men.

"Who are you?" one of the Russian Policeman asked.

"Cywiak," I said.

"What are you doing out so late?"

"I'm coming home from a job. I'm a painter and had a long day's work. I just want to go home now."

"I'm afraid we can't let you, you have to come with us."

"Why? Where are you taking me?"

"You're needed for an important job detail."

"The canal?" I asked. They didn't answer, but their silence was confirmation enough.

They escorted me towards the train station along the top of a hill. I knew I needed to get away or I'd never see my family again. I would probably die working on the canal.

At one point, I doubled-over feigning injury, so they let go of my arms, thinking I was in trouble. In one motion, I shot up and jumped over the edge of the road and down into the wooded valley below. I tumbled down the hill and got a little banged up, ended up with some bruises, but nothing serious.

It was pitch black by then. They couldn't see a thing, so they did not try to follow me.

Once again, I escaped certain doom.

Not long after, while at work, I was picked up by the NKVD again. They were different officers this time. As we trudged toward the station to board a train for the canal construction site, I decided to take a bold risk.

We approached a large house along the road, which I recognized as my supervisor's house. My guards did not appear to be too bright. I pleaded with them to allow me to enter the home, so that I could announce that I would not be reporting to work anymore.

They gave me permission, so I quietly entered the house. Nobody was there. I walked to the back of the house, opened a window, and jumped out, leaving the NKVD men waiting.

26

Later that same year, there was a loud pounding at our door in the middle of the night.

"Cywiak! Come on out, Cywiak!" It was the NKVD looking for me! They had learned who I was and where I lived.

My wife and I lived in the house with her sister and mother. They shared one bed and Malka and I used the other. There wasn't much more in the house aside from the beds—there was no place to hide. I didn't know what to do. We looked at each other with frightened expressions.

And then it hit me.

I got inside the bed and had my wife, mother-in-law, and sister-in-law all lay on top of me. It was the only option—there was nowhere else to hide, no way to escape.

When they forced the door open, they only saw three terrified women huddled together on a bed. I couldn't see the Russian Police, but I could hear their boots clomping against the floor as they began to approach the bed.

"Where's Cywiak? Where is he?"

"He's not here," my wife answered. "He's working."

"Where is he working?"

"Well, we don't know where he's working. He works all over the place, wherever he is needed."

"Needed to do what?"

"Paint buildings. He is a painter."

"Uh-huh. When is he due back?"

"I don't know. He's been gone on a long assignment."

They wanted to find out as much as they could about me and where I was, so they could grab me and force me to work on the canal.

Not very long after that close call, the NKVD found me as I headed for work and arrested me. They escorted me to their office building and threw me into a small room. They made me turn in my clothes and gave me a uniform to wear instead.

Stuck in this room, I was not sure what was in store for me, but I was reminded of a story.

Moses Maimonides, also known as the Rambam, was the private doctor of the Egyptian king. He was a brilliant man. Not only was he a doctor, but he was a rabbi, philosopher, and one of the greatest Torah scholars.

One day the king was riding on the street in a horse and buggy. He took a right turn and suddenly he saw the Rambam walking by.

He stopped and said, "Ahhh, Moses, how you doing? Where are you going?"

The Rambam said, "I don't know."

"What? Moses, the Rambam, the big doctor, doesn't know where he's going? I can't believe it—are you making fun of me? You're lying to me! I'm the king of Egypt!"

The king got mad and ordered for the Rambam to be taken away to be thrown in jail. Overnight, the king started to feel bad about the whole thing. There must have been a reason, he thought, He never made fun of me before. He must've been teaching me a lesson! I better go to the jail and see how he's doing.

The king went to the jail and approached the Rambam.

"How are you doing, Moses? You feel good, you feel comfortable?" he joked.

"As comfortable as possible."

"Well, that's the way it is. Look, Moses, you cannot fool me. There must be something. Why did you say that you didn't know where you were going? It doesn't make any sense—you know exactly what you do. Everything you do, you know what you're doing."

The Rambam said, "Why do you say that? Did I know that I was going to be taken to jail? How could I know that?"

The king was correct—it was a lesson. Nobody knows what could happen to them in the next minute.

I certainly didn't know what was going to happen to me when I was on my way to work before the Russian secret police picked me up.

The door to my room in the NKVD office building was left unlocked quite often, but there were many guards around the building who would recognize me in the prisoner's uniform. Since I was permitted visitors while in captivity, I got word to my wife to bring me some clothing. She brought them in a briefcase and convinced the guards that she was bringing me some food, so they allowed her to leave the briefcase with me.

As soon as she left, I put on the clean clothes that she had brought me. The clothing was quite nice and formal; something Malka must've found at the consulate. I tucked the briefcase underneath my arm and left the room.

My heart almost went out of my chest. A group of guards were sitting outside the building, and when I came outside, they all stood and looked right at me.

I didn't realize until I was past them that they were standing at attention when I passed. They mistook me for an NKVD official!

27

Since the Russian Police were after me, I decided to get a job outside of town and stay there until things calmed down. I knew that my wife and family would be okay, since they were after me, not them. And although he'd have to be careful, Moishe could look in on them to make sure they were doing well.

I arrived in a town and found out there was a coalmine. I started working there to earn some money for food. Really, I wanted a job in the city where I could steal something useful, but what could I steal from a coal mine? I couldn't even find a way to transport coal!

Plus, I worked underground and the air was very bad; I couldn't breathe too well. It wasn't working out for me, so after one of my shifts, I left for the day and didn't come back. But I couldn't find any other work in that area, so I went back to the mine and thought maybe I could bribe somebody to give me the better job, one that was *above* ground.

I found the man in charge and handed over some cash. Sure enough, he gave me a good job; no longer did I have to work underground. Instead, I worked at the weigh station. When the coal came up, it would be loaded into trucks. I would calculate how much the truck weighed before and after it was loaded, so we knew how much coal was aboard. After I completed weighing the truck, it transported the coal to its destination.

When taking a job away from home like this, unless I knew of a friend in that area, I usually paid rent to stay at a house. That was the case while I was at the coalmine. Since it didn't pay well and there was nothing to steal, after several months working there, I finally walked away from the job.

Still looking for work in the same city, I happened across a big family with a lot of sons. They were all shoemakers. They were well off and had a huge home. To be a shoe maker was good, because all the Russian officers and generals needed nice boots. These generals and officers had the money to pay, so this family was able to make a lot of money with their business.

The family was very nice and welcomed me into their home for a while. These people recognized my name and knew a lot about my family. Not only did they know that my father was a popular rabbi and the principal of the Hebrew school, but they knew my grandfather's reputation as a well-known rabbi, cantor, and mohel. They considered it an honor for me, a rabbi, son and grandson of these great rabbis, to be a guest in their home.

I wasn't too surprised that our name was recognized. My grandfather, especially, was very well known throughout Europe.

28

My grandfather had been tall and macho. Very broad and strong. He could pick up big objects as though they weighed nothing. People used to say that with one hand, he could pick up all sixty-three books of the Talmud, in one big stack, without even straining!

He was a different kind of rabbi from my father. He had lived in the same city as us and also had a job with the community, but he was a kosher meat inspector in Wyszków. He would go to the slaughterhouse and if the meat qualified, he would put a stamp on it saying that it was kosher. Owners of some of the slaughterhouses would give him the lungs, livers, and hearts from cows. The lungs especially were not the best food, only the poor people would buy these. But he got them for free. That helped a lot to fill up the stomach. My grandmother used to give them to my mother to feed our large family.

His other job was as a "khazn," a cantor, and he got paid well for that. As a tenor, he had a great big voice, but very smooth at the same time. Yom Kippur was the biggest singing service of the holidays. People used to say that when my grandfather started to sing "Kol Nidrei," a popular song sung at the eve of every Yom Kippur that means "All My Vows" in English, the windows of the hall would vibrate with just his first two words.

I never got to hear him, because I used to go to the services with my father to see the Gerer Rebbe, where somebody else did the singing. But my grandfather's synagogue belonged to the city—it was for everybody. It was a giant synagogue. There were no microphones in those days, but he didn't need one. His voice was that *powerful.* That's why they gave him the job, because they needed someone who everybody could hear in a hall that big.

He may have made his living from inspecting meat and singing, but he was also a mohel. He had circumcised me and my brothers. In Wyszków, he circumcised everybody there. He was famous. Nowadays, most rabbis are afraid to be mohels for the fear of making a mistake during the procedure and getting sued; it could affect the rest of their lives.

My grandfather refused money for the circumcisions that he performed. Not only didn't he accept money, he also brought a big cake, which my grandmother made, and a bottle of sweet wine to make the blessing, to every circumcision. He donated this for each procedure.

Everyone had a lot of respect for him. He was like a rebbe, not just a rabbi. My grandfather was different from the people now. We don't get this type of treatment anymore. Hitler eradicated much of this kind of true, Hasidic kindness.

Possibly the only place that may still show some of that type of true generosity would be in Israel, where it is possible to find the truly righteous people. A righteous person like this would be called a "Tzadik," but when referring to a group of people like this we call them "Tzadikim." There were many more Jewish people like this before Hitler. Nobody wanted to be criminals or bad guys. They didn't want to be a "Racha," an evil person. They wanted to be good; the best they could be.

I had many different teachers as I grew up, and they were all true Tzadikim. It was very rare to find a rabbi who was not a Tzadik. They were different from everyone else, *very* different. Their souls were dedicated to doing and being good, and teaching others to be good—that's all they lived for. They had a lot of influence on me and the man I am today. These people created a righteous environment.

There were beautiful books, which talked of nothing but morals and ethics. Crime? What crime? They didn't even know what a crime was—how could people be criminals? They couldn't even think about it. Everything that came out of people's mouths was always nice and good . . . such great warmth. Some people think it's impossible for a Jew to be such a good, generous person—not true! It is possible—they all used to be like this.

Hundreds of years ago, if someone went into a Jewish community, all he would find was Tzadikim. All the Jews throughout the world were generous like that. Where do we see it now?

Those days and acts of generosity are long gone . . . and we'll never see it again.

Hitler destroyed it all.

29

The shoemaker's house was beautiful and immaculate. Everything inside seemed valuable. I remember passing in front of a fancy mirror on their wall as they gave me a tour of their home. I was shocked at how thin I was. This was the first I had seen myself in years. My face looked sunken in, my cheek bones protruded, and I realized that I could definitely afford to gain a few pounds.

I don't know why, but looking at myself in the mirror reminded me of an old story, and I began to laugh out loud.

"What is it, what's so funny?" the shoemaker asked. His family was all around with curious looks on their faces.

"Your mirror reminds me of a good story," I said.

"I'm sure we'd love to hear it."

"Okay, well there was this young, recently married couple in a small shtetl, like the one I'm from. The people in this town were not used to modern conveniences. Most of them did not even *know* what a mirror was, let alone what one looked like. They didn't have them.

"The husband was Orthodox; very religious. He used to go to the big city to buy merchandise for a store he owned. During one trip, he bought a mirror as a present for his wife Freda's birthday. He gave it to her as a wrapped gift and said, 'This is for you—I thought you would like it.' He didn't wait for her to open it; he just left and headed off to his store to work.

"While he was gone, Freda opened the present to see what it was. She looked at it with confusion at first—she didn't know what to make of it. She'd never seen herself before, so she had no idea she was looking at her own reflection. She thought it must be a picture of someone. Suddenly, Freda started crying and crying. 'Oy vey! A terrible thing has happened!'

"Her mother lived upstairs. So she hurried down and said, 'Freda, what are you crying for? What happened?'

"'Look, mother! Look what he brought me! He brought me a picture of a beautiful woman, whom he fell in love with in the city. He's going to want a divorce and leave me for this woman.'"

"The mother looked in the mirror and said, 'What are you, crazy? This is a picture of an old woman! She's not even pretty! There's no *way* he left you for her.'"

We all had a good laugh, and if they didn't already love me then, they certainly did after that.

I stayed at the shoemaker's house for some time. The father was the main shoemaker and his sons all helped. He also had a daughter, and she was a beautiful woman at that. She always treated me very kind, constantly smiling and asking if I needed anything. She would drop what she was doing in a heartbeat to help me with something or make me something to eat.

I soon realized that the mother and father wanted me to be their son-in-law. They wanted me to marry their daughter. They didn't say this openly, but I knew it. They treated me like a king there. Oh, they didn't know what to do with me! Even before the war, they had hoped to have a rabbi for a son-in-law. But in those days, during the Holocaust, it was not easy to find a young, single rabbi.

Of course, I was already married by then, but they didn't know this. And I didn't tell them, because I had to take care of myself. They were helping me, giving me "papa", Polish for food. And good food at that! I tried to keep my distance from the daughter, because I didn't want her to find out the truth . . . and I certainly didn't want to lose the papa!

The smell of the food alone was to die for—I hadn't smelled anything that good in many years. It was the best food we could get in those days. They had the money to buy whatever they wanted in the market; meats and all. Being a rabbi, I didn't eat meats, not even if they were kosher. But it didn't matter—all of their food was terrific.

I liked the nice home, kind treatment, and good food, so I stayed with them and began to gain a little weight back. I had only been with them around a month or so, but I got strong again. Then they openly came out and said they wanted to have a wedding and have me marry their daughter.

I said, "I'm sorry, but . . ."

"But what? You like it here, right? Don't you like our daughter?"

"That's not the problem. You see, I'm already married."

That was it. I had to leave the house right away.

Getting attention from women during those times was not unusual. The war took away every young and middle-aged man to fight in the Russian military. I didn't go because I was a Byezcyenyet; they didn't trust me in the army.

I was a young man, and every woman looked at me. I was always hungry and on the run before I settled and got married, so I rarely had the desire for women then. I didn't have the strength and didn't need the intimacy. I was more concerned with basic survival.

The Russian military left a lot of women alone and *they* needed intimacy; *they* wanted male companionship. Many of these women had experienced good lives, wives and girlfriends of high-ranking military men.

But with the war against Germany, all the men were gone.

30

I returned home to Andizhan and learned that the search for men to work on the canal project had ended. I was able to get some painting jobs for Russian military officers. Those became great jobs, because they fed me. They knew I was hungry and wanted me to do a good job painting their homes.

Eventually, I was recommended to a man named Zurbin, the chief of the secret police. He was the head man. I wanted to make sure I did a great job for him, because I knew if I did, he would take care of me, and I could help take care of my new family.

May was their big Communist holiday. The 1st of May was the date the Communist party took over Russia. Zurbin had a nice big house and wanted me to paint it for him, inside and out. The government gave them big salaries, gave them everything, so money was no issue for him. I painted his whole house in time for the holiday celebrations. And he was thrilled! He gave me food for every meal I was working. He also gave me some other things, like paintings, to take home.

Better than the food and the paintings, his best payment to me was a document. Zurbin put a red stamp on my papers that said BRON. That meant security for me. With that symbol, the secret police couldn't punish me any longer; they couldn't touch me.

Before when I walked down the street, I had to be worried that they were going to stop me and send me away to slave labor or Siberia. Now if approached, I just had to show them my paperwork with the BRON, and they would leave me alone. After that, nobody ever bothered me again.

Back when the Germans first declared war against Russia, the majority of the Russian soldiers did not even believe in Communism. They were not going to sacrifice their lives for Stalin. What kind of life did they have under Communism?

They weren't really free. They couldn't even get enough food to keep them alive, so they had to steal to get by. What were they fighting for? So they surrendered. That's why the Germans were able to go so deep into Russia in such a short time. They didn't get much resistance.

Eventually, the Russian soldiers realized that Hitler and the Nazis were going to be even worse than Stalin! The Nazis were just killers. They killed all the people who gave in. The Russian soldiers soon learned that surrender was not an option.

Starting in the woods with the partisans, they fought back. The Russians were good fighters. Also, the Nazis were more focused on killing Jews at their death camps, than fighting in the war. If a Nazi soldier wasn't doing his job properly, his superior would threaten to send him to the Russian front. They were more terrified of fighting the Russians than what their fate would be for murdering Jews.

The Russian army gained confidence with the stand at Stalingrad, and eventually Russia started to win the war. Since the Russians had already lost much of their military and were tired and weak, the Americans supplied them with weapons, tanks, and supplies, everything they needed to continue taking the war to the Germans. With this aid, they pushed the Germans all the way back to Germany, and were the first ones to reach Berlin, even before the Americans and English.

The United States and Russia hit Germany from both sides. The United States and its allies came in through Italy, and Russia came in through Poland and Czechoslovakia. Together, they crushed the Germans. In Berlin, Hitler secured himself and his closest staff in his bunker. When he knew he had lost the war, he and his longtime girlfriend and recent wife, Eva Braun, committed suicide together.

✡ ✡ ✡

On December 12th, 1944 my first son, Chaim, was born. In 1945, when my son turned one year old, we planned a big party. We received news on that same day that the war had ended! We had a big celebration. We were so happy that the war was finally over after all these years. And, my son turned one. He represented the future.

There was no immediate change, though. We still had to work. The struggle to survive continued. Russia was in a poor state from the war.

Part IV

Road to Freedom
(September 1945 - Present)

31

In 1946, the Russian government started the process of returning us to Poland. It was a long process, but eventually I was returned to Poland with my wife and son, a year after the war had ended.

At first the Russians transported us to a city that used to be occupied by the German military, but now belonged to Poland once again. The Germans, knowing the Russians were on their way, had evacuated the city and left thousands of empty houses there. There were no people in this city. The Russians rounded up all the refugees from Siberia and other places in Russia and dumped us all there.

While staying there, an announcement came on the radio for all surviving rabbis to head to the big city of Łódź, Poland, and join a new rabbinical seminary, which combined the survivors from all the other seminaries. There were nearly one thousand Jewish yeshivas in Europe before the war, and now we would gather to form the only one remaining.

The surviving rabbis and yeshiva students were to meet at a synagogue; the only one in all of Łódź that had not been destroyed. It was a small, privately owned synagogue that was probably spared because it had been hidden in the corner of the Łódź ghetto and used as a warehouse for salt.

Before the war, many beautiful synagogues existed in Łódź including the famous "Great" Synagogue. The Nazis demolished four well-known synagogues during a five-day period from November 10-14, 1939. Empty squares had taken their places.

I was instructed to take the train and go to Łódź by myself and meet all the others at the synagogue. My wife and son had to stay behind for a short time.

In Poland, long before the war ended, a group of anti-Semitic Poles called the "Super Patriots" gave the Jewish people a hard time. They protested against us, intimidated us, shoved us, and at times, even beat us up. They were like the Nazis, but not nearly as big, organized, or strong. The Polish government didn't officially support their beliefs.

The Super Patriots were a political party. They tried to win the government by votes, but they didn't have anywhere near the following that the Nazis had. They had just enough support to make a lot of trouble for the Jewish people.

The Super Patriots had a Polish slogan: "Jews, go to Palestine!" They used to scream it in the streets to intimidate the Jews. This was happening before the war, but, as we'd learn, Hitler's examples gave the Super Patriots more freedom to act out with violence.

When I got to the train station to begin my journey to Łódź, I heard a rumor that the Super Patriots were out to kill Jewish people. In the middle of the night at train stations, they would search the passenger cars and look for Jews. They would pull them off the train and kill them in cold blood.

Supposedly it was happening on some trains, but not all of them. I had no choice, though. I was risking my life, but I needed to get to Łódź.

As soon as I got on the train, I hid under a bench. It just so happened that at the next stop, a group of these Super Patriots came aboard with rifles, and they rounded up any Jew they found. Terrified, I curled up in a ball, trying not to move a muscle or even breathe if I didn't have to. The people sitting around me—the ones who saw me go under the bench in the first place—were Polish. They could've told these anti-Semites where I was, but they didn't. I laid down there during the entire ride.

The Super Patriots removed eleven Jewish men from the train. From under the bench, I couldn't see anything, but I could hear the shots. They were all killed. In my worst nightmares, I couldn't imagine this happening. The war was over and we were survivors, returning to our homeland.

Those eleven men survived Hitler and the Nazis, only to be murdered in cold blood after the war, by a group of anti-Semitic Polish citizens. More senseless murdering of Jews.

When I finally arrived in Łódź, I learned that only around three hundred fifty rabbis and rabbinical students had made the journey. That's it! Out of the tens of thousands of rabbis and students that had lived and worked throughout Europe before the war, we were left with three hundred fifty.

Our goal was to get out of the country, because Poland was being controlled by Russia. Because it was the Russian military that had forced out the Germans, they remained in control as though Poland was their country. Their military presence was responsible for allowing a Communist Polish government to be created.

Once I realized what the future plans were, I was able to bring my wife and son to Łódź as well. The sad part was that we had to part ways with the rest of her family, including my good friend, Moishe Tryzmel.

We waited for an American Jewish organization to take us out from Poland. In 1939, an organization called Vaad Hatzala was created in New York, with the purpose of saving surviving rabbis and students training to become rabbis. A very famous Orthodox rabbi, Eliezer Silver, from Cincinnati, Ohio who helped organize Vaad Hatzala, was named their president.

While we were in Łódź, the United States government sent Rabbi Silver to Poland. To protect him from the Russian government, he was given the honorary military title of an American general. They gave him that title so the Russians would respect him and allow him to do the job he needed to do. The Russians *had* to respect the American military; they were now allies. Rabbi Silver was free to move around like a representative of the United States government.

Rabbi Silver brought millions of dollars stuffed into valises with him. The United Jewish Appeal, who funded his mission, is an international organization that helps Jewish people who are in need or in harm's way. They still exist today and help any Jew wherever he or she lives. They give Israel monetary assistance as well.

Even though the United Jewish Appeal financed Rabbi Silver's mission, Vaad Hatzala handled all the logistical details; they arranged all the visas and planned the trips. The Yeshiva University of New York gave me a scholarship, so that I could get my visa to the United States.

Rabbi Silver used the money from this fund to bribe the Communist government, their immigration department, the soldiers who controlled the borders, and anyone else they had to, in order for the Russians to let us go.

He succeeded.

It took six months to get us out of Łódź. They gave us our own passenger train to go to Czechoslovakia, which was also controlled by the Russians.

In Prague, the capital of Czechoslovakia, we stayed in a hotel for a few months while negotiations continued. I found out from staff that the mattresses in those rooms were stuffed full of human hair that had been sheared from some of the six million Jews who perished in the Holocaust. I could not sleep on the mattresses. The thought of it made me sick.

I slept on the floor.

The biggest obstacle wasn't getting into Czechoslovakia; it was in going from a Communist Czechoslovakia to the free Democratic country of France, which was controlled by the Allies.

The Russians at the Czechoslovakian border had to be bribed because their laws told them not to let *anybody* in or out of the Russian borders.

After three months in Prague, an agreement was reached. We were given permission to travel to Paris, France.

We were finally moving towards freedom!

32

In France, we were free people. Completely. We had all the conveniences of a democratic society. Finally we were able to live like normal humans.

We were housed in the countryside, a small farming village called Bailly, about fifteen miles west of Paris. Like in Lithuania, we were back to studying like nothing happened. We were to be the rabbis of the future! We studied the Bible and the Torah, but mainly the Talmud and the many books of Talmud scholars.

On the first Saturday, the first Sabbath of the month, we always had a nice meal. I used to go in a rented car to Versailles, the next big city, to buy live chickens for the meal. We would kill them according to our laws and make chicken soup for Friday night and Saturday.

One time when I made the journey, a delivery truck slammed into my car. My body was bruised and I lost almost all of my teeth, which had to be replaced with dentures.

After the accident, I was lying in bed recovering when I had a surprise visitor. Label, my oldest brother by ten years, walked into the room.

"Label, you survived?! I never thought I'd see you again!"

He didn't have much to say, but his expression showed the pain and trials that he had endured. I did not ask him for details and I would not share mine.

"But the rest of our family is gone," I said with sad reflection.

"Nahum made it!"

"Really? It has been so hard thinking that I was the only survivor of our entire family. Is he all right?" I asked hopefully.

"Yes, he survived in Warsaw. And now he's turned religious."

"How about that. Nahum, found G-d after the war. I am glad for him. How's your family?"

"We're doing well. We have two boys and two girls now. I see that you have a son of your own."

I smiled. "Yes. He is a good boy. How did you find me?"

"A friend heard of your accident and recognized the name. I wanted to come see if you were all right."

"I survived the war—I can survive this too."

He said, "So glad you did," he said. "After all you've been through to survive the war, it would be a real shame if a car accident did you in."

We gave each other a grin and a handshake. The years between us, the war, and our spiritual paths bound us but separated us. We visited a short time, careful not to discuss anything of importance, the wounds all too deep and too fresh.

Label would go on to run a successful synagogue in New York. Nobel Peace Prize winner Elie Wiesel, who had survived Auschwitz to become a very successful author, professor, and political activist, was a member of Label's congregation.

Yes, since only my teeth had been damaged from the car accident in France and the rest of me was basically unharmed, I marveled at G-d's grace again. I had bones like iron—unbreakable! And my legs were strong from all the walking and running and jumping I'd had to do over the years.

Once again I was spared.

Another miracle.

33

We were in France for over eight months. We had to wait for our paperwork and passports to be created. Any proper identification we had before the war was lost, stolen, or destroyed during the Holocaust. It took a long time to get the Visas and travel arrangements worked out. Everything had to be coordinated between the Polish, French, *and* American governments. My visa was based on a scholarship of the Yeshiva University of New York to study for a higher ordination, like a Ph.D.

There were hundreds of us to worry about, and everyone had problems, so we couldn't go anywhere until the paperwork was done for the entire group. In the meantime, we continued with our studies.

We shipped out from the port of Cannes, France, across the Atlantic Ocean, towards the United States on a Polish boat called "Sobieski."

The ship was small, which made the journey to the USA very rough. We were packed on the ship like sardines and people were vomiting. Such a long voyage in those conditions, but eventually we cruised into the New York Harbor late at night. It was dark and we couldn't see the Statue of Liberty, but we were in the free land of America!

The ship sailed straight to Ellis Island. We all had to wait on the boat until morning. My wife and my son stayed close by my side. In the morning we still had to wait on the boat in a long line while one by one, we were registered at Ellis Island. I had a single visitor. A rabbi named Tzvi Bronstein, who was from Wyszków and had studied under my grandfather.

He was a very important guy in New York by then. Not only was his name well known in New York, but all over the United States. He was a mohel, and had learned the craft of circumcising from my grandfather in Wyszków, Poland. Many years before the war begun, he had left Poland and moved to the United States.

During the war, he had worked in the United States Army as a chaplain, circumcising soldiers. This was often necessary if they had problems due to the filthy conditions they found themselves living in. The military sent him all over Europe, wherever they needed him to perform. There was a big need for those skills.

Once Rabbi Bronstein found me, he stayed with me all the time. Every day, he would pick me up in Brooklyn, where we both lived, and drive me to the Bronx. It was a long ride. He took me to the Lebanon hospital where he worked. After the war, he opened and operated a school there to teach rabbis how to circumcise babies. This is where he taught me how to do circumcisions. I practiced hard and once my skills were perfected, he gave me work to do.

He told me, "Now's the time I can repay your grandfather."

The first circumcision I performed was on my own son, Chaim. Originally he had been circumcised in Russia by an old rabbi, who shook. He was a very old man with a big white beard, and he did a bad job with Chaim. He was so old, his hands were too unsteady.

The old rabbi only removed a little piece; he didn't do the whole thing. The rest, the head, was still covered. That's not kosher; that's not the proper method of circumcising, but at the time we had no choice because there was nobody else to do it. He was the only rabbi who was also a mohel in that part of Russia.

In New York, we had to do Chaim's circumcision all over again. He was already two and a half years old by then. This time with me doing the procedure, it was a success!

In the sixty plus years since, I've performed over six thousand circumcisions. It may not seem like a lot over the course of sixty years, but for me, it was plenty of work!

34

My second child, our daughter Rebecca, was born during my first year in New York. While learning to be a mohel with Rabbi Bronstein in the Bronx, I continued working towards my rabbinical education in Brooklyn.

My rosh yeshiva, Rabbi Yechiel Mordechai Gordon, from my rabbinical seminary in Łomża, Poland, was lucky enough to come to America about six months before World War II broke out. He came to New York at that time to raise money for the Łomża Yeshiva, but once war broke out, he could not go back. People had to convince him to stay in the United States—he was not the kind of rabbi who would run away from his people, especially when they were in need.

Everybody loved Rabbi Gordon. He was a great teacher, very brilliant. There were rabbis who studied under him at the Łomża Yeshiva and moved to the United States afterwards. These former students of his, who thought fondly of him, helped him to come to the United States, but once he was forced to stay, they helped him settle down and begin earning a living.

Rabbi Gordon had a big house in Brooklyn. The second floor was his home, the main floor was the synagogue, and the basement was for the classrooms to run his yeshiva, which he also named the Łomża Yeshiva. When many students came to America, including me, we studied at his yeshiva.

I began studying towards a higher ordination because I wanted a deeper, broader rabbinical education. Another reason I needed to study was that I lost the papers with my proof of semicha in Russia, when everything was stolen from me on the train. Since I had to work for a new semicha anyway, I figured I may as well study for the higher ordination, because I already had the knowledge for the standard rabbinical ordination and doing the work just to regain my certification would be a waste of efforts and resources. The new semicha would be like a PhD—very prestigious in the rabbinical world.

I started training immediately in Rabbi Gordon's seminary in Brooklyn while I was also learning how to circumcise babies. I didn't get to finish seminary right away, because I was offered a good job in Louisville, Kentucky that didn't require the title of Scholar.

My rabbis, whose names were impressive, gave me a letter that stated I was working towards my title of Scholar and, I was qualified for the job.

Louisville offered me $1,000 a month, which was good money in 1948! My family was growing, so I couldn't turn it down. The community wanted me there because not only was I a rabbi and a mohel, but I was also a khazn and a "balkora," meaning I could read Torah scrolls. I could also be a supervisor of kosher laws. I had most of the skills of a Scholar.

The Louisville position needed to be filled as soon as possible, so we packed up our possessions and, with my wife Malka and our two young children, I left for Kentucky right away and we stayed for six years. During that time, my daughter Bernice was born. Since Louisville did not have a Hebrew day school, I had to leave when my son Chaim grew to that age.

After Kentucky, I took a job in Jersey City, New Jersey, which is close to Brooklyn, New York. In Jersey City, our fourth and final child, my son Baruch, was born.

On one terribly cold day with lots of snow on the ground, I circumcised Baruch at the synagogue. Rabbi Joseph Soloveitchik, the chief rabbi at the modern orthodox Yeshiva University, was the "Sandik" for that ceremony, meaning that he was the one to hold my son while I performed the circumcision.

While I was working in Jersey City, I was able to continue my studies to become a Scholar, which I eventually received in Brooklyn, New York by the "av beth din," literally meaning Father of the Court, Rabbi Natilowich. In total, it took me twelve years—from 1947 until 1959—of study to reach this level of semicha. And even though the title of Scholar is similar to a Ph.D., it's important to remember that Ph.D.'s can be acquired in roughly eight years. A great deal of time and study was required to receive my higher ordination.

Rabbi Gordon, who was very popular in Europe, was a fairly newcomer to the United States, which is why he did not sign my semicha. He wanted to make sure I had the name of a popular American rabbi on my semicha. Rabbi Gordon was a great man and a good friend, and really wanted to help me out. He wanted to arrange for me to meet with the great Chief Rabbi Moshe Feinstein. I told Rabbi Gordon that I would be honored to, but not until I felt prepared.

Rabbi Gordon was almost at the same level as Moshe Feinstein, but Moshe was so brilliant and was known all over the world. He was also quite humble; he never wanted to be called Rabbi Moshe, just Moshe Feinstein. I felt nervous and wanted to make sure I was ready. I would spend the next three years continuing to study, so I would be ready to meet with him.

Before that meeting, I was offered the job as Principal Rabbi in Caracas, Venezuela in 1960 at the Union Israelita de Caracas, which was strictly an Orthodox synagogue. For my job at the Union, I needed the title of Scholar and the timing for everything worked out perfectly. In Caracas, I was the Principal Rabbi for a large community. The job paid very well, but it wasn't easy. It was a big responsibility.

In 1963, I finally found the courage to meet with Moshe Feinstein, and returned to the United States to do so.

I met with him and he was very happy for my successes. He asked me a lot of questions; gave me a test to see if I was properly educated. My responses convinced him that I was.

Moshe Feinstein wrote and signed a special letter, and in this letter was his "ascama," agreement of my Scholar ordination, and his high recommendation, which stated that the synagogue in Caracas was very fortunate to have me as their Rabbi.

Moshe Feinstein died on Purim and every year for the past thirty years since his death, he's been honored on Purim. Many articles are still being written about him, today.

To give you an idea about what kind of man Moshe Feinstein was, I remember this powerful story about him.

There was a journalist, a religious Jew, who wanted to do an article on him. It just so happened that his aunt was Moshe Feinstein's doctor. His aunt set it up so that her nephew would meet Moshe during his next medical appointment with her.

After the appointment, the doctor had another patient to tend to. She said "Goodbye" and gave Moshe a kiss on the cheek! The journalist began to tremble. It was unheard of for a woman to kiss a holy man like that; it's against traditional laws.

He apologized profusely, "Rabbi Feinstein, I apologize. My aunt, she isn't frum *[religious]. She doesn't understand..."*

Moshe placed his fingers on the man's lips to prevent him from speaking, and then in Yiddish, softly told him something that nobody ever said before. "She has numbers on her arms. She is holier than me."

It's a very powerful statement. And maybe, like the survivors of Auschwitz; the ones like me who had to fight for years to stay alive, sleeping in trees, stealing food, living in the rottenest of conditions to escape certain death many times, are also considered holy for the long struggle we fought day after day just to survive the Holocaust and resume the life of an observant Jew.

My cousin, Rabbi Shlomo Goren, was Chief Rabbi of Israel for three terms from 1973 until 1983. The *only* person he ever trusted when seeking guidance on religious law was Moshe Feinstein. This demonstrates just how much respect and trust others had in him.

Moshe Feinstein was very special, and I was fortunate to have his signature on my title. The semicha itself is not signed by him, only a special letter testifying that he agreed with my receipt of this title. He certified that it was accurate and that I was to be considered a Scholar "Without Limit." I would have the right to put my opinion anywhere, and my writings could become law.

Today, rabbis don't have the time to study the areas necessary to reach this level of semicha. They have other areas of study they need to devote their time to. They are very learned in their own right, but the roles of this generation's rabbis have changed since the time I reached my highest level of ordination.

While serving as Rabbi in Venezuela from 1960 to 1992, I was able to do very important work in Caracas. Before I had arrived in Caracas, there was only one synagogue, the Rabinato de Venezuela. Unfortunately the president and treasurer of the synagogue acted like a dictator. Many of the congregants were unhappy, so they left, hired me, and formed the Union Israelita de Caracas.

Upon my arrival, a very large percentage of the congregants from the Rabinate joined me at the new Union Israelita de Caracas, despite the fact that we did not even have a synagogue. For those first couple of years, we rented a house in town where we met and held our services. During that time, we were having a brand new synagogue built for us. Once it was finished, I had the honor of blessing the first stone of the building.

During my first eight years at the Union Israelita de Caracas, I was the only rabbi at the synagogue, and the congregation grew more during this period than any other years in its history.

After that eight year period, I was authorized by the Union to look for a rabbi fluent in speaking Spanish, who could relate to the new generation of congregants. This was absolutely necessary! I hired Rabbi Pynchas Brener, and worked with him at the Union for another four years.

Later, I took a job at the Rabinato de Venezuela, which was also strictly Orthodox, where I was the Principal Rabbi for another fourteen years. By this time, the dictator who had been president and treasurer when I had first moved to Caracas had been forced out, so now the synagogue was run democratically. 1,350 congregants from the Union followed me over to the Rabinato!

We had a huge synagogue with a lot of members. During the holidays we had to open the doors and connect it with the big hall; we needed the hall space to fit in thousands and thousands of people!

I received and still possess letters from the "rabbinates," a governing body of rabbis, of both Jerusalem and Tel Aviv, which gave me the full authority to make a rabbinical court in Caracas and make decisions on the laws of religious subjects. They also gave me permission to appoint two witnesses to join this court.

Not only did I appoint two witnesses to help with this big job, but I also made sure these witnesses were rabbis, so I would have two assistant rabbis to help me out. Together we held a court for all types of cases such as divorces, conversions, etc. We were a permanent court of three rabbis, no jury. The three of us judged the cases and our decisions were final.

I was also the Honorary Rabbi at the San Cristobal Community Synagogue, fulfilling their religious needs when requested during my entire time in Venezuela.

During my years in Venezuela, I was decorated with honors from the government by two different Democratic presidents. First, I received a third grade honor, the Francisco de Miranda order, from the president of Venezuela, Carlos Andres Perez, which came in the form of a golden pin. Later I received a second grade honor from President Luis Herrera Campins, which was a special sash worn over the shoulder and across the chest. I left before I could receive a first grade honor, the highest esteem that could be received by a civilian from the Venezuelan government.

While in Caracas, I was able to help Moishe Tryzmel and his family to come join us there. After the war, they had been able to leave Russia, but they'd gone to Bolivia instead of the United States.

So once again, my friend and I were reunited.

By then Moishe had a wife named Luva, and a son they named Aviv. Aviv is still alive and living in Caracas to this day. He is on the board of directors at the Rabinato de Venezuela.

Some years after the Tryzmels moved to Venezuela, my mother-in-law, who had moved to Israel after the war, became ill. Our youngest son Baruch was grown and staying in Israel at that time. Malka went to visit her mother to help out.

While she was over there, I received a phone call from Baruch. My dear Malka, while caring for her mother, had unexpectedly died of a heart attack.

It was such a shock, and I was devastated for quite some time. All we'd been through to survive and raise a family, and suddenly she was gone. Our children were grown and on their own by then. I missed Malka very much.

I suspect that the harsh conditions Malka had faced while in Siberia had contributed to her death. Sometimes such extreme duress can never be overcome.

Years later, on May 1st, 1979, I married my current wife Rukmini, who's Hebrew name is Rachel. She was one of the secretaries at the synagogue, and had attended Hebrew Day School in Chile. Her son, David, whom I had circumcised as a baby, was seven years old when we married.

In 1992, I moved to St. Augustine, FL to be the principal rabbi at a beautiful synagogue called the Sons of Israel Synagogue. As a volunteer, my wife, Rukmini, has been giving Hebrew lessons at our synagogue for the past nineteen years.

Shortly after arriving in St. Augustine, I started running a conversion course for, among others, those who are interested in converting to Judaism. The course takes nearly a year to complete and its content is guided. At the end of the course, men and women seeking to convert appear before the Bet Din. Serving the Bet Din are three people, the rabbi and two witnesses. If the convert is found to be suitable, he or she undergoes ritual immersion. If the convert is a man, the Brit Milah and the Hatofas Dam Brit Milah are required, as stipulated by Jewish Law.

All conversions are based and done according to ירה דעה הלכות גרים, pages 661, 662, and 663, and also according to the גמרא יבמות, pages 46, 47, and 48, starting at ת"ר, the last nine lines at the bottom of page 46.

In the year 2000, I received a lifetime contract from Sons of Israel. After being a rabbi for over sixty years, I'm finally set to be retired by June of 2011.

Epilogue

Why did G-d pick me? Why did He pick me to survive and experience all these miracles? Why did I survive when my father and the other elders were gunned down in the woods? Why did I escape the ghetto, the invasion in Lithuania, the Communists attempts to catch me? Why did I not get spotted by the Super Patriots on the train?

Why me and not someone else?

I have a theory, a belief about this. My father, who was a righteous person, had to die for those who were not so righteous.

This may not make sense at first. Surely the way he led his life secured him a good place in heaven. Those people, like my father, grandfather—who were both rabbis—Rabbi Wasserman, Rabbi Bronstein, Rabbi Gordon, and Rabbi Feinstein, really just people, would have some respect in heaven. And their prayers would be powerful.

So, let's say that after my father died, he was up there in the right place and he prayed to G-d: "Please, G-d, I want my son to survive."

And G-d listened to him. Why? Because my father was a righteous person. Because he died for somebody else. So G-d felt that He should answer my father's prayers, not for me, but for my father. Perhaps a person who lives a just life will have his prayers answered, even if it's for someone who has not yet lived that just life.

I believe this could be one explanation.

Where did I come up with this belief? From the Bible. The story of Rachel, the wife of Jacob, who cries to G-d endlessly for the children, her children, the Jews. She mourns for us being exiled from our land, for our pain and suffering over thousands of years. She's always praying for G-d's blessing over us.

Prayer reminds G-d that we're here. If I'm not worthy of having my prayers answered by G-d, he will answer them for Abraham, Issac, and Jacob, our forefathers.

He answers them for Rachel.

He answers them for my father and grandfather, who I knew personally in life.

He does it for them for they are the just, the righteous, the ones deserving to be rewarded.

For a survivor, who has already experienced many miracles just to survive, everything with faith starts making more sense; it's our own, unique journey. Family is nearest to our body and our heart, so it's hard to accept their loss, but we begin to realize there is a plan in everything, even if we don't understand it.

Many people can't understand how G-d could have let the Holocaust happen. Why didn't He interfere and prevent Hitler and the Nazis from carrying out such terrible atrocities?

Because of free will. Regardless of the act of evil, if G-d interferes and punishes a person right away, they lose their free will. G-d would be dictating everyone's actions. People would have to be careful and be good all the time, but they would be *forced* to be good. And G-d would become a dictator. This is the reason I can give for why G-d did not interfere with the Holocaust.

But that explanation is still not good enough for a survivor. Why didn't G-d make just this one exception? Six million murdered Jews? One and a half million of them being children? Wouldn't sacrificing man's free will be worth it to save all those innocent children? It makes the free will argument hard to swallow.

But is it hard enough to doubt G-d's existence?

Many people question "faith." Even I questioned it during some of the horrors I witnessed during the Holocaust. But I can't explain my survival, my success, in any other way. Someone was always watching over me, protecting me. Someone larger than any human in this world.

But what about the people who have not experienced all these miracles? Who may have had many bad things happen to them? How are they to believe in what cannot be seen?

Let's say I found a letter on the street and opened it. I read it over, it's a nice letter. I don't know who it's from, but I *have* to believe that it's from *someone*. *Somebody* wrote this letter. It didn't mysteriously create itself! Ink didn't fall out from a bottle and pour onto a piece of paper to form words and sentences to become a nice letter, all by itself.

Well, the same applies to the earth, the universe. How can anyone think these things were created on their own? That there wasn't a creator behind all of it? How could anyone not think that things like babies, nature, and so much beauty on earth didn't come from a greater power?

As humans, we're limited. There's only so much we can do. With all of these unexplainable phenomena and miracles that have happened, how can we claim responsibility for it? We are limited, but G-d is unlimited in what He can do.

He can make the impossible possible.

He can make miracles happen.

I'm living proof.

What I Have Learned From The Holocaust

For fourteen years, five times a year, I have had the students of Flagler College in St. Augustine, FL come listen to my story at the Sons of Israel synagogue.

One time, a female student asked me, "Did you ever wish you had been born a Christian, so you wouldn't have had to experience the Holocaust?"

I said, "Look, it's a good question and it probably went through my mind at the time. Why not, it makes sense . . . if I was a Christian, I wouldn't have to suffer and lose my family. But . . . would I really want that?

"To be born a Christian or something else? What if I was born in a family of Nazis? They bring me up to be a Nazi. And I could've ended up killing Jewish children. Could I have done that? Could I possibly wish for something like this? Of course not."

The girl opened her mouth, but didn't say anything. Not a word.

There are several lessons that I've learned through my experiences in the Holocaust. The first is that religion is like fire.

Karl Marx once stated that, "Religion is the opiate of the people." Opiate being a narcotic that dulls the senses, forcing lethargy and apathy.

But I don't agree with his philosophy. I say religion is like fire and fire can be a good thing. It can keep you warm and you can cook food with it to keep you fed and healthy. Of course, fire can also kill you. It can burn your house down or destroy an entire city.

Fire can be good or bad depending on how it is used.

Religion is like this. It can be used for good or bad. Doing something beneficial in the name of G-d is good. Helping others, having faith and belief, obeying the Ten Commandments, are all examples of how religion can be used for good.

Religion can be used for bad as well. Like the killing and terrorism in the Middle East. So many wars have been fought in the name of religion. Why? Religious people are supposed to be benevolent, not violent. If you take *anything* to an extreme, you can be burned.

Too much religion can be just as dangerous as too little religion. The best example I can give is the blind faith the Hasidic rebbes had that G-d would not allow Hitler and the Nazis to do all the horrible things they threatened they would do. They believed that Messiah would come and save us all.

Of course, that did not happen. The Hasidic rebbes were wrong! General Jabotinsky, the non-religious leader of the Zionist movement, had insisted that the Nazis would murder us, and urged us to leave Poland and Europe. We should have listened to Jabotinsky and fled!

In this case, religion was literally like fire. Many millions of Jews were burned in the death camp furnaces, because of our failure to flee from the Nazis.

Aside from General Jabotinsky, the well-known and respected Vilna Gaon was also against the Hasidic movement from the beginning. This was more than one hundred fifty years before the Holocaust. He feared their blind faith would cause tragedy down the road and he was right.

The Hasidic rebbes were not considered lawmakers in the Jewish community. They did not have authority over Jewish law. They weren't discriminated against, but the non-Hasidic people were against Hasidic philosophies and interpretations.

The Vilna Gaon respected the Hasidic people. He considered them to be good Jews, but he disagreed with their all-or-nothing beliefs. All of the Lithuanian seminaries were against these beliefs as well. Before the war, there was only one, true Hasidic seminary in all of Poland; it was in Lublin.

Even though there were millions of Hasidim, they did not have the educated rabbis to support their movement and help them to get financial backing to build seminaries.

The Vilna Gaon's respect of the Hasidic people was carried forward to the rest of the misnagdim, who were against the Hasidic beliefs. We followed the wisdom of our elders when considering how we felt about the Hasidim.

There is a book, *The Wisdom of Our Forefathers*, which teaches us how to handle disagreements. It tells the story of two brilliant scholars, Shami and Helil, who were good friends and highly respected each other. Despite this, they disagreed on many things. But these debates were healthy and in the name of G-d. Helil was more liberal, so people often sided with him.

Rabbi Moshe Feinstein and his good friend, Rabbi Yosef Eliyahu Henkin, were very much like Helil and Shami. They often disagreed and had debates on various issues. A popular debate they had was about divorce. Rabbi Henkin believed that if a Jewish woman was married in a non-religious court and lived in a non-religious marriage, she needed to be divorced by a rabbi—which is a lengthy procedure—before she can be married again. Moshe disagreed. He believed if a woman was not married in a synagogue by a rabbi, then there was no need to be divorced by a rabbi, she could do so through a non-religious court. This was to make it easier for a woman to get remarried. Most agreed and sided with Moshe. Not only was Moshe a brilliant scholar, but also a humanitarian.

Rabbi Henkin resembled the role of Shami, primarily extreme or conservative in his thinking, while Rabbi Feinstein was more like Helil, leaning toward the liberal point of view. Like how Moshe commented that the doctor who kissed him was holier than he was because she had a number tattooed on her arm from the Auschwitz death camp. That was a liberal thing to say, because by Jewish law, women simply are forbidden to do such a thing!

The Vilna Gaon was also like Helil in his opposition to the Hasidim. He was liberal, but peaceful in his debates, which is how the misnagdim acted in turn.

The misnagdim respected the Hasidic Jews and accepted them as part of the Jewish community. Unfortunately, there was no mutual respect. The Hasidic Jews discriminated against us. They discriminated against their own women, not allowing them to participate in many areas. This attitude caused a lot of problems with the Jewish communities and even created problems within individual families.

Even now, the Hasidim are mainly students of the Torah and Talmud, and they remain as students. Most of them don't have jobs. They receive funding from the government to live the life of students. The Hasidim are also protected by the government from being drafted by the military. They don't contribute towards Israel. They don't volunteer themselves for the Israeli military or for the betterment of the Jewish community or for the state of Israel.

The Hasidim did not learn from the Holocaust. A Hasidic rabbi once personally told me that a synagogue where women and men sit together is not considered Jewish anymore. And, based on his beliefs, those congregants are not considered Jewish either and could not step into a non-Hasidic synagogue, which, in my opinion, is a serious mistake.

The Hasidim ignore the Talmud, in particular in the Gemara סנהדרין "Sanhedrin," a volume from the Talmud, where it says that a Jew who sins still retains the identity of a Jew.

They ignore how the Torah teaches us that we are not supposed to add a new law or take away from any Jewish law!

The second lesson that I've learned is that money, too, is like fire. The Torah says that even Tzadikim, "righteous people," can do wrong because of money.

Deuteronomy 16:19 gives a fair warning of this, "Do not accept a bribe, for a bribe blinds the eyes of the wise and twists the words of the righteous."

Even today in our faith, we have those who make mistakes because they are blinded by the appeal of money.

Greed has caused too much death and destruction on this planet. The Nazis were after the wealth of the Jews during the Holocaust. Look at the lengths they went at to acquire it!

Some people are not satisfied with just being rich. They have an unquenchable thirst to acquire more and more money. This is affecting the Jewish community as well. The extremists are allowing greed to dictate their beliefs. They are changing tradition and faith for the selfish reason of gaining more riches and power.

I have experienced this sort of greed head-on at one point during my sixty-plus years of being a rabbi. One of the services that I perform is converting people over to Judaism especially for those who want to do "Aliyah," moving to the State of Israel, to protect and help Israel.

Many years ago, some rabbis in a community I worked at began to say bad things about me. They lied and spread words of hate. They told people that I was a Reformed rabbi. This was done to scare all the Orthodox rabbis, in particular the "Chief Rabbanut," our most supreme religious governing body in the State of Israel, so that they would not recognize my work as a rabbi.

They were angry with me because I was only charging a very small amount of money for each conversion, compared to the large sums of money—even in the thousands of dollars—that Orthodox rabbis wanted for the same job.

I charged so little as a special favor for the big groups of people who did Aliyah to help and fight for the state of Israel. I worked in conjunction with an Israeli agency and a couple of their "Shaliach," representatives of Israel. Israel needed as many converted men to help with their military as possible, in part to make up for all those Hasidim who didn't join the military. For the betterment of the Israeli military to protect our land, I wanted to make it affordable and desirable for people to do Aliyah and convert to Judaism. Besides these people had already been living by the Jewish laws for over five years while waiting to convert over, so I felt obligated to help.

The rabbis who resented and hated me didn't care about this, or even respected my level of semicha. They were upset because with my much lower and more reasonable rates, I was taking away their business, preventing them from becoming rich.

One time, there was a rich Jewish man who was to marry a non-Jewish woman. Their rabbi wanted an exorbitant fee to handle the future bride's conversion before he would marry them at their synagogue. After they spoke to me, I offered to do the conversion for $1,000, a mere fraction of their rabbi's fee. I did so, but their rabbi no longer agreed to marry them at their synagogue.

Only the money and the prospect of becoming rich was important to him.

The third lesson is that the Holocaust could have been prevented if the state of Israel had existed during the times of Hitler and the Nazis.

Because of the Holocaust, I consider myself to be an Orthodox Zionist Rabbi. I had agreed with Jabotinsky. But the Hasidic movement was opposed to the beliefs of the Zionists. If the Zionists would have had more support from the Jewish community, and other countries in the world, we could've had our nation much earlier.

After the Holocaust, the Zionists would eventually make Israel a strong country with a powerful military. I believe that if today's Israel had existed in the days of Hitler, the Holocaust would never have happened.

Israel's army would have done anything necessary to fight the Nazis and save the Jews from being mass murdered, like they did in 1976 when they rescued Israeli and Jewish hostages who were being held at an airport in Entebbe, Uganda by Arab terrorists.

The fourth lesson I've learned is that there were great Hasidic rebbes, like the Gerer Rebbe, who were more Zionist, than Hasidic in their beliefs.

The Gerer Rebbe was saved from the Holocaust because he desired to go to Palestine to help build the state of Israel. There were other great Hasidic rebbes who did not wish to go to Palestine. They preferred to go to the United States.

The early Hasidic movement was founded by Rabbi Israel ben Eliezer, the "Ba'al Shem Tov," back in the 18th century in present day Ukraine. Despite the Vilna Gaon's efforts, the Ba'al Shem Tov movement grew in popularity and over the years produced many rabbis who were great, great people, much like the Vilna Gaon.

Moshe Feinstein was on the same level as the Vilna Gaon was in his time. The way Moshe learned was the same way I had. And these lessons that I've learned from the Holocaust, I've learned from Moshe Feinstein.

The last lesson I've learned is that rabbis need to be prepared against any attempts of violence against them. Not to be singled out and murdered like the rebbes during the Holocaust. Or to be victims of terrorism like some synagogues and Jewish centers around the world are experiencing in the present.

Rabbi Gary Moskowitz, the president of the Tzedek Task Force on Counter Terrorism, believes that rabbis and their staff should be armed and trained to use weapons at their synagogues. He hosts training sessions at various New York-based synagogues.

Although this is not a popular concept among many rabbis, I agree with Rabbi Moskowitz, based on my experiences during the Holocaust. How could a survivor feel any differently than this? Especially since acts of violence are still happening at synagogues. Why should anyone become victims if they can avoid it? If offenders know that we are armed, they will not come after us.

I mean no offense to some Jacksonville rabbis who are opposed to this idea, but most of the Jacksonville synagogues are better protected with more security. The Sons of Israel synagogue, where I preside, is right off a public street with no real protection at all. Our front door is a short distance from the curbside. The lack of security for us is worrisome.

Rabbi Moskowitz believes that several people should be armed near the entrance to the synagogue, and if someone threatening comes in with a gun, these protectors should kill him. A lot of our synagogues are defenseless from attack. Anyone could just walk in with a weapon and do great harm to us and our congregations.

It's a law from the Torah. If somebody comes to kill you, you better kill them first. Even though the Torah is very much against killing, it makes this exception. It's your obligation to defend yourself and the rest of your people.

At ninety years old, I feel I'm too old to learn how to use and care for a gun, but these young rabbis, especially if they make a good salary, have every reason–and every justification-in the world to want to protect themselves.

Hopefully we will never forget what happened during the Holocaust, and can take heed of the severe lessons to be learned.

The selected elimination of a group or civilization can never be allowed to happen again. Yet the Jews are already facing such extreme hatred. Instead of Hitler, there are other evil men doing his work.

Some Arabs say that Jews are killing Arab children to drink their blood, just like a handful of the Polish Christian priests said before the Holocaust. These Arabs are now putting it in their newspapers and teaching this to their children at school. They're saying that the food for Purim is made with Muslim blood.

Similar injustices are happening in other countries through anti-Semitic leaders, just like Hitler, contaminating the minds of their followers with false claims against the Jews. Hate spreads easily. If we're not careful, history will repeat itself!

Another Holocaust is not impossible. That's why we need to be extra vigilant in preventing this type of discrimination and hatred from happening again.

We're all followers of the same G-d, so we should all be able to get along together and be good to each other.

Hatred is not what G-d teaches.

Glossary of Foreign Terms Used

Aliyah - Moving to the State of Israel.

ascama – An agreement of a scholar or rabbinical ordination.

av beth din – Literally means "Father of the Court." A highly respected rabbi and most senior jurist.

balkora – One who can read Torah scrolls.

Byezcyenyets – Russian for refugee.

cantor - A Jewish official who leads the musical portion of a service.

chavrusa – A study-partner at a yeshiva to help engage in intense Talmudic studies.

cholent – A stew with meat, potatoes, and vegetables eaten for lunch during Sabbath.

Jude – The German word for Jew. The plural form is **Juden**.

Kaddish – Prayers for the dead.

kapusta – A Polish soup with either cabbage or sauerkraut.

khazn – A Jewish cantor.

Kol Nidrei – A popular song sung at the eve of every Yom Kippur that means "All My Vows" in English.

Kristallnacht - Literally translated to "Crystal Night," this was the first organized attack by the Nazis on the Jewish people living in Germany and Austria and occurred November 9th and 10th of 1938.

Lost Ten Tribes - Ten of the original twelve Hebrew tribes who created the northern Kingdom of Israel.

Midrash – In-depth commentaries and interpretations on the Hebrew Scriptures.

minyan - A group of ten Jewish adults required for some of our religious duties.

misnaged – Individuals opposed to the Hasidic beliefs, a movement; also called the Lithuanian system, founded in the 18th century by the Vilna Gaon. The plural form is **misnagdim**.

Neshamah - Hebrew for soul.

NKVD - The Soviet secret police.

Oy vey - A Jewish expression of woe or exasperation.

papa - Polish for food.

Pidyon Ha'Ben – Ceremony for redemption of the first born son.

Chief Rabbanut – The State of Israel's most supreme religious governing body.

rabbinate – A governing body of rabbis.

Racha - An evil person.

Rashi - A French sage and genius, who is most famous interpreter of the Talmud.

rebbe - A Hasidic leader.

rosh yeshiva – The dean of a rabbinical seminary.

Sabbath – Or Shabbat is the seventh day of the week, Saturday, and is the Jewish day of rest and worship.

Sandik – The honorary person holding a child while a circumcision is being performed.

Sanhedrin - A volume from the Talmud.

semicha – An ordination of a rabbi. There are increasing levels of ordination, similar to progression in academic degrees.

Shaliach - Representatives of Israel.

shalom - Traditional Jewish expression of greeting or farewell.

shtetl - A small Jewish village

Super Patriots - A group of anti-Semitic Poles who lashed out with violence and murder against Jews who survived the Holocaust.

Talmud – The collection of ancient rabbinic writings consisting of the Mishnah (base of the Talmud containing six subjects on Jewish law) and the Gemara (the many interpretations of the Mishnah) that constitute the basis of religious authority in Judaism.

tefillin - A pair of black boxes with leather straps that contain scrolls of parchment inscribed with Bible verses. The straps of the tefillin are wrapped around the arms and head during morning prayers of observant Jews.

Torah – The first five books of the Hebrew Scriptures.

Tzadik - A righteous person. The plural form is **Tzadikim**.

yeshiva – A rabbinical seminary.

Related Websites:

www.FlightFromFear.com

www.JeffSwesky.com

www.DreamerPublications.com

CPSIA information can be obtained at www.ICGtesting.com

234994LV00001B/2/P

9 781937 100001